HOW TO MAXIMISE YOUR PROPERTY PORTFOLIO

MARGARET LOMAS

Wrightbooks

Also by Margaret Lomas
How to Make Your Money Last as Long as You Do
How to Invest in Managed Funds
How to Create an Income for Life

First published March 2003 by Wrightbooks
an imprint of John Wiley & Sons Australia, Ltd
33 Park Road, Milton, Qld 4064
Offices also in Sydney and Melbourne

Typeset in 11.5/13 pt Minion Regular

Reprinted with revisions and tax updates November 2003

© Margaret Lomas 2003

National Library of Australia Cataloguing-in-Publication data:

Lomas, Margaret.
How to maximise your property portfolio.

Includes index.
ISBN 0 7016 3759 5.

1. Real estate investment. I. Title.

332.6324

All rights reserved. No part of this publication may be reproduced, stored in a retrieval system, or transmit ted in any form or by any means, electronic, mechanical, photocopying, recording, or otherwise, without the prior permission of the publisher.

Cover design by Rob Cowpe

Printed in Australia by McPherson's Printing Group

10 9 8 7 6 5 4 3

Disclaimer

The material in this publication is of the nature of general comment only, and neither purports nor intends to be advice. Readers should not act on the basis of any matter in this publication without considering (and if appropriate, taking) professional advice with due regard to their own particular circumstances. The author and publisher expressly disclaim all and any liability to any person, whether a purchaser of this publication or not, in respect of anything and of the consequences of anything done or omitted to be done by any such person in reliance, whether whole or partial, upon the whole or any part of the contents of this publication.

Contents

Special dedication

I would like to dedicate this book to my much loved father. Dad always read my manuscripts before they were published, but sadly he passed away unexpectedly before this one was ready. He set an example for me and taught me to strive to be the very best I could be. His confidence in my abilities served to motivate and inspire me. He was truly a great man.

To my wonderful family

My husband Reuben, who stays true, caring and supportive
no matter how rough the terrain becomes.

My son Mark, for his humour and positive attitude.

My daughter Kristy for her perseverance, energy and
commitment to life.

My daughter Belinda, a joy to behold who
lights up everyone's life.

My son Michael, who cares deeply about us all
and shoulders all our burdens.

My daughter Rebecca, whose goal setting and sense of justice
will see her successful in all she does.

Thank you Steven for the care you give to us all.

Thank you to my mother and father for being there
and encouraging me.

And lastly to my brothers and sisters who continue to put up
with me and encourage me always.

Since my first book *How to Make Your Money Last as Long as You Do* was released, there has been much heated debate, even argument, over the best and most profitable way to invest in property. Prior to its release, little was known about the concept of investing for cash flow—it seemed commonly accepted that property investors did so for the sole purpose of realising a large gain upon eventual sale, after which they would spend their lives in the lap of luxury, reaping the rewards afforded them by their genius. Often, the price for this gain was the pain of losing money each week as inevitably returns on this sort of property rarely provided enough funds to pay associated outgoings. Property investors accepted that this shortfall would be met from their own pockets and satisfied themselves with the small reprieve provided by the tax advantages this contribution could bring.

When Robert Kiyosaki began to warn investors against any investment requiring a cash input, effectively espousing that positive cash flow was an absolute must, few property investors realised that this also applied to them. Negative gearing had become the catchcry of high-income earners all over the country, and it seemed that this wonderful concept of positive cash flow, however much sense it made, could not be applied to property.

There were, however, the smug few who, perhaps unintentionally, had chosen property which did in fact deliver this elusive positive cash flow. These investors were enjoying the benefits of property ownership without the often daily stress of finding that extra $50 or so a week to support the property. Unwittingly, they had acquired true cash flow investments, often more than one, and they quietly accumulated more and more property, waiting for the time when they would retire from the paid workforce and live off the rental income.

I recall clearly when I first realised the value to me of a positive cash flow investment property. My first property typically cost me around $45 a week from my own pocket, and this was at a time when my children were small and the budget could ill afford any further beatings. I had increasing equity in the house in which I lived but could see no way that I could leverage this as I had no cash left to support another property, even when interest rates were at an all-time low.

I literally fell across a property one day which had exceptional rent return for the purchase price. By my calculations, this particular property could deliver something like $60 a week into my pocket, even taking into account a possible low occupancy. I remember sitting down and going through the list of why I wouldn't buy this property, and the only thing that kept cropping up was that I could not be sure of the growth potential. But then I began to realise that I could not be sure of the growth potential on any property I was to buy. My budget was so tight that even if the absolute guarantee of huge capital gain was presented to me on a platter, I would be unable to take advantage of it anyway! Far better to at least have a property which, although it may not grow so fast in value, would continue to deliver a return, than to have no property at all.

As it turns out, this very property is one of the greatest performers in my portfolio, having almost tripled in value in just three and a half years. I could never have guessed this—and certainly none of the so-called experts I consulted at the time predicted this huge growth. But, even if it had not experienced this exceptional capital gain, the property delivered on its promise of great cash flow and this cash flow afforded me the opportunity to reduce debt and so leverage again anyway, even without the growth.

Property investing does not take any great talent—but it certainly takes a whole lot of common sense. And while the debate rages on about when and where you should invest, and with what aim (cash flow or capital gain) you may well be wasting time if you are sitting back waiting to see who is right. If you accept that everyone may be right and then think about what is right for you, you can decide for yourself which method of property investing suits you best.

In the past year and a half, positive cash flow property has virtually become the buzzword of the investment scene. Clever marketeers have seen the opportunity to use this concept (with few truly understanding what it means) to sell their property, and discussion rages on websites and in property clubs all over the country. Yet still confusion prevails, and every day more and more questions are asked.

As I become more skilled with my own investing and ask more and more of the right kinds of questions myself, I also become more informed and more able to assist others to do what is right for them. And, despite having now written two books on the subject, every day new questions are asked that no one has thought of, or at least verbalised, before.

How to Create an Income for Life not only told investors what to do, it provided easy-to-follow steps and a how-to strategy for investors. It has turned previously novice investors into skilled, thinking strategists. However, as with most things, it still raised questions, mostly from those investors who already had a few properties under their belt, and hence the need for another book.

And so to this book. I hope *How to Maximise your Property Portfolio* brings answers to many of the in-depth questions I am asked every day. I hope it gives all investors the ability to critically consider their own portfolios and make wiser decisions in the future. Of course, this may not be the last book! No doubt, no matter how thorough I try to be there will be something else that comes up after the release.

It would be beneficial (though not essential) for you to have read my other books before starting on this one. In them, you will find detailed descriptions of just how to recognise and buy positive cash flow property. You will find important information which I am not going to repeat in this book.

But, before you do read on, a quick word of advice. Investing should be fun. It should be exhilarating. It should not be the cause of sleepless nights and endless worry. There is little point to planning a profitable retirement if the journey is so filled with trauma that you die before you make it! Open your mind to the possibilities, enjoy the ride and not only will you prosper, but you will grow happy and healthy as you grow old.

Margaret Lomas
margaret.lomas@edestiny.com.au
Glenning Valley, NSW
March 2003

1 The positives and the negatives

❏ Property as an investment is different to other investments

❏ Investors should be seeking positive cash flow at all times

❏ Negative gearing may mean loss to the investor

❏ On-paper deductions may turn a negative cash flow property into a positive one

At the risk of repeating myself, it is important to start at the very beginning (a very good place to start!). I can hear the moans of the experienced investor—*not another protracted explanation of positive cash flow!*

No, it won't be, but certainly we must lay the ground rules by restating the differences between property and other investing, and clarifying the three ways that returns can be obtained if you have chosen to make property the vehicle for your investing future. If you are already a full bottle on this subject, skip ahead to the next chapter. Otherwise, you might wish to be sure that we are all starting on the same page, so to speak.

Property as an investment

If there is going to be a debate about which type of investment provides the best return over time, count me out. It is a little like the eternal question—where did it all begin? There is no easy answer and you could spend your life in this debate and no one would ever win.

As an investor, I choose property because it suits me and I like it. As a financial adviser, I will categorically state that if you are to obtain the greatest possible investment return with the least possible amount of risk, you must spread your investing over each of the asset classes. In an ideal world, we would all have beautifully balanced portfolios with a mix of property, shares, cash and fixed-interest investments, and no debate would be required. Now let's take a look at reality.

In real life, the majority of income earners, particularly in the middle stages of their lives, have little or no spare cash. It is all they can do to make ends meet today, what with the expense of children and their daily lives to consider. The Great Australian Dream dictates that we must, at all costs, buy a home of our own, and the pressure on young people to do so is enormous. Supporting this dream can be a nightmare for those whose income stretches only as far as the monthly mortgage repayments. Add to this the fact that all around us we are vigorously encouraged to lessen the burden on our national debt by planning for our own future, and it is no surprise that we have a huge portion of the population whose last thought is of obtaining an investment portfolio at all, let alone a balanced investment portfolio.

The true yield on any investment must be weighted by its risk factor

For those who do decide to take the plunge, the issue is further muddied by the vastly different views of investment experts. Share investors would rather die before they touched a direct property investment, while property barons accumulate tangible assets and claim that there is no other way.

In truth, there are two important factors to consider. Firstly, it is not an equitable process to compare assets from different classes with each other. This is because the risk factor of every asset class, and every asset type within each class, varies widely. The true yield on any investment must be weighted by its risk factor, and since it is almost impossible to measure risk with any mathematical expression, it is also unfair to compare two different assets with each other. While it may be fair to say that ABC shares outperformed XYZ shares in any one period, you cannot possibly say that the return on ACME managed funds at 10 per cent for the year is a better return than the 7 per cent a three bedroom house in Centreville has shown. This is because the risk factor for ACME managed funds is different to the risk factor attached to the three-bedroom house in Centreville.

The second and perhaps most compelling factor which governs where you ultimately invest is, of course, your personal cash position. While few people have actual cash lump sums to invest, many, many people quickly and often inadvertently build equity in homes they live in and are paying off or own, and this equity can provide the leveraging power to invest further in more property. While it is true that the same property equity can provide the funds required to purchase any kind of investment, it is a reality that many people feel more comfortable using bricks and mortar to buy more bricks and mortar.

Failed property investments almost always relate to the failure of the investor

People choose property for a wide range of reasons, including:

☐ many people feel property is simple and does not require any great financial skills

☐ it is a tangible asset the investor can see and touch

☐ it gives the investor the sense of having some control— the investment is not left in the hands of fund managers or company directors

☐ it often allows for easier access to financing, with banks and other lenders offering a vast array of loan options which are not at call

☐ it can be sold in a generally deep market (albeit not a highly liquid one) in the event that liquidation is needed, with a constant supply of buyers in most cases.

As a nation of property owners it is only natural that many of us would also choose property as an investment vehicle. Failed property investments almost always relate more to the failure of the investor to use efficient purchasing strategies and carry out the requisite amount of due diligence rather than the failure of property itself to deliver sound yields.

Property returns

When we consider property as an investment, it can be difficult to measure the actual returns you are receiving on that investment. While you may take the rent into account, to gain a true picture you must also consider not only any gain you make upon eventual liquidation but also the costs of investing over time. This includes the cost of the lost opportunity to invest elsewhere, which is particularly relevant where your property purchase has required a steady cash input from your own pocket while you have owned it.

Regardless of whether you are buying property in the hope of making a grand profit upon sale, or to set up a retirement income which will continue long after you have chosen to leave the paid workforce, you will be receiving a return, or yield, while you hold the property. Whether the property costs you money each week or provides after-tax dollars in your pocket will depend on whether the property is negatively geared, positively geared, or positive cash flow. Let's briefly examine the differences between the three.

Negative gearing

This is the term most commonly used to describe any property that is geared (which means that loan funds have been used to purchase the property) with expenses on the property outweighing the actual income made on the property.

Usually, a negatively geared property is one where 100 per cent or more of the purchase price has been borrowed. While an investor cannot simply borrow more than the purchase price, use the excess for any purpose they like and claim the lot as a tax deduction, it is allowable for an investor to borrow all of the money he or she needs to complete the purchase and claim the interest portion of the loan funds used for the purchase. This may include costs for conveyancing, valuations, loan establishment costs and any other cost which is legitimately incurred for the purposes of purchasing an asset designed to earn an income. Consider the following example of a negatively geared investor:

> Neil bought a 25-year-old property worth $150,000, borrowing $158,500 to effect this purchase. In addition to the $10,778 (at 6.8% pa) in interest repayments he had to make, he had a further $2,000 a year in rates and other costs. His rent return for this property was $150 a week and, assuming a 50-week per year occupancy rate, this resulted in a return of $7,500 a year. As Neil's expenses exceed his income by $5,278 a year and he pays tax in the 30% tax bracket, Neil gets back $1,584 in tax from the tax department, which somewhat offsets his loss. In total, Neil must pay $71 a week from his own pocket in order to keep this property.

[handwritten margin note: pd $100 toward it after tax deduction = $70 per week]

Negative gearing has been popular for many years now and most of us know of someone who has property such as this. The effectiveness of this strategy will be compared to other strategies at various stages in coming chapters.

Positive gearing

As the name would suggest, positive gearing is the opposite of negative gearing. It is where the raw income on a geared property exceeds the raw expenses and no cash input is required from the investor. Clearly, all investors would choose positively geared property if it were as simple as this. However, there is usually some catch and there is definitely no such thing as a free lunch. Positive gearing can only occur where the rent return on a property is higher than the national average for the purchase price (which is 0.1 per cent of the purchase price as a weekly rent amount), or where an investor is less heavily geared—that is, borrowing less by bringing in cash of his or her own.

Take Jean and Phil as examples:

Jean had $85,000 from an inheritance. She purchased the property next door for $150,000, borrowing $73,500 to cover the shortfall between her cash and the purchase price plus costs. Her rent return was $150 a week for 50 weeks a year, or $7,500. Her costs were $4,998 in loan interest and $2,000 for rates and other costs. Jean's income exceeded her costs by $502 and as she is also in the 30% tax bracket she must pay tax on this gain of $150. This leaves Jean with $6.75 a week in her pocket.

Phil was lucky enough to find a property in an area where the prices had not yet soared, but rent returns had steadily increased in the past. So, rather than receiving the usual 0.1% return on purchase price as a weekly rent, he saw 0.175%, or $262.50 a week ($13,125 for 50 weeks), on the property costing him $150,000. He borrowed the full purchase price plus costs, and so paid $10,778 in yearly interest on the total loan of $158,500. His other costs totalled $2,000. His rent return exceeded his costs by $347, resulting in tax to be paid of $104 (assuming a 30% tax rate). Phil is left with $4.60 a week in his pocket for this investment.

These are both highly viable examples. The major problems for many investors, however, would be that few of us have lump sums to invest as Jean had and if we did a $6.75 a week return for this size investment (not including any sale profits) would seem a very small return. In Phil's situation finding property with such a relatively high return is a little like trying to find a needle in a haystack—it can be done but it may take a long time! A viable, positively geared property is one of those things which may come around once or twice in your investing lifetime. If it does and everything else stacks up, it is a potentially profitable investment for you.

Positive cash flow

Positive cash flow property involves a more technical and financial approach to buying property. It involves knowing enough about the tax laws to be able to choose property which falls within the allowable dates for claiming a range of on-paper deductions.

To keep this simple, if you buy property built after September 1987, you are allowed to depreciate the original costs of construction at the rate of 2.5 per cent over 40 years (known as 'special building write-off'). In addition to this, you are allowed to claim the depreciating value of any furniture, fixtures and fittings which are included in the property (but not a part of the actual building) at varying rates according to the type of item and its accepted effective life. Chapter 5 takes an in-depth look at the kinds of items you can claim. Once you understand more about the list of possible claims, you will more clearly be able to see the impact this can have on your net cash position.

> Peter bought a six-year-old property for $150,000, borrowing $158,500. The original construction cost for this property was established by a quantity surveyor as being $75,000. It was fully furnished and the total value of furniture, fixtures and fittings was $30,000. The loan interest was $10,778 and the costs were $2,000. The rent return for this property was $150 a week, for 50 weeks a year, or $7,500 per annum. In addition to the raw loss of $5,278, on which Peter received $1,584 tax back (at the 30% tax rate), he also was able to make a claim for $1,875 in special building write-off and $12,000 in year one for his first year's depreciation on the furniture, fixtures and fittings. This resulted in more tax back to the tune of $4,163. In total, Peter received $7,500 in rent plus $5,747 in tax back (totalling $13,247) and paid out $12,778 in total costs. His net return is $9 a week into his pocket.

Peter bought a property with standard rental return, but due to the on-paper deductions he has been able to obtain a positive cash flow. This example is just one of many ways that on-paper deductions can either assist to turn a negatively geared property into a positive cash flow one, or reduce the tax payable on a property where the rent returns are more than the expenses.

If Jean and Phil buy properties with allowable on-paper deductions, they may effectively (on paper at least) wipe out the taxable gain and so benefit from the cash flow without incurring additional tax. If Neil was to ensure that his purchase carried on-paper deductions, he may well wipe out his loss and receive back enough tax to cover the commitment from his own pocket that is currently required.

This is not to say that all property built within the allowable dates can be magically turned from property with negative cash flow into property putting money consistently in your pocket. It also does not mean that a property which shows a positive cash flow in year one will stay that way every year. There will still be an abundance of property with a rent return so low in relation to the purchase price that no amount of on-paper deductions can change this. If you do decide to purchase property despite the fact that it will have a negative cash flow, it should only ever be due to an absolute conviction that, over time, huge capital gain will make this investment pay off for you.

On-paper deductions mean that, with careful research, a little more knowledge and an abundance of energy, you can take much of the stress and financial hardship most people expect from property investing out of the equation. This will enable you to put together a relatively safe and quite well performing portfolio which—although it may not break any records in terms of its growth—will deliver attractive and stable returns over time and allow you a comfortable retirement.

Summary

❒ You cannot compare property returns to other investment returns unless you can weight the risk factor by some measurable mathematical formula.

❒ Many income earners have no spare cash to invest, and would rather use home equity to buy more property than 'paper' investments such as shares or managed funds.

- ❏ People choose property because they feel more capable of understanding it.

- ❏ Property offers returns via negative gearing, positive gearing or positive cash flow.

Conclusion

Mary wrote to me some months ago and outlined the extent of her property portfolio, which at that stage was considerable. Although her portfolio was performing quite well, she really had little clue as to what she actually had in it. In fact, she had quite a mix of properties but she was not sure which ones were the most effective and where she should go next.

This had nothing to do with Mary's intelligence—she had a responsible position as an attorney in quite a large law firm. It had more to do with the fact that, as a busy person, Mary had placed her trust in those people selling her the properties to guide her in her investment choice. As she had not taken the time to fully understand important concepts, the success of her portfolio had a lot more to do with luck than with anything else—but just how much longer would Mary's luck hold out? Judging by the number of other emails I get with outcomes not quite this good, I would say that Mary is very close to making mistakes which may impact markedly on her portfolio in the future.

Maintaining your portfolio and ensuring its effectiveness over time is a skill every investor must learn

There are many important concepts which you must understand both before commencing and while managing your property portfolio. Understanding the differences in the available cash flows on property is only step one. Once you have learnt to recognise the potential of any property to deliver a consistent cash flow, there is much more work to be done. Maintaining your portfolio and continuing to ensure its effectiveness over time is a skill every investor must learn. The ability to question, analyse and then adjust any portfolio, be it property or otherwise, is the vital tool which will keep your investment performing to its best potential, whatever the economic situation and whatever your own personal financial circumstances.

2 The great debate – cash flow or capital gain?

❐ Property investors will choose cash flow or capital gain when investing

❐ The cost of investing for the growth investor is usually negative cash flow

❐ Cash flow investors usually cannot afford to commit personal funds to their investing strategy

❐ There are costs and benefits to each method of investing

Back in the olden days, the only reason people made investments of any kind was because they wanted to get an increase on their original investment. When a farmer bought a cow, it was in the hope that this cow would produce more cows, and so the investment was leveraged, which in turn resulted in more money. The farmer happily delayed the use of his money (that is the purchase price of the original cow) and even committed more money (the upkeep of the cow) in the hope that this one cow might produce more cows, which could be sold for profit. The benefits of this type of investment did not materialise until the cow(s) could be sold.

The concept of buying company shares made the process of investing more complex and, at the same time, more (or less)

profitable, depending on the ultimate success of your choice. In buying the share, the hope of the investor was to not only benefit from the gain possible upon sale, but to also benefit from cash flow along the way in terms of the dividends received in the event that the company traded profitably. This added another dimension to investing and made the pain of going without the money for the term of the investment a little more bearable.

When people first began to buy property as an investment, many of them used cash to do so. As lending against property as an investment in the early days was very rare and certainly not easily accessible by an individual, the concept of leveraging did not often apply—each property was purchased after enough cash had been saved. The returns came in the form of the weekly cash flow (the rent) and the eventual capital gain upon the sale of the property.

Over the past 20 or 30 years, there have been some notable events in the history of property price rises. In my own lifetime, we have seen the property boom of the '80s. At that time, I sold a townhouse I owned for just $38,000, only to find it worth some $80,000 no more than six months later. Many people owning property as an investment during this time prospered, selling quickly before the plateau and making seemingly impossible gains in short periods of time. It was around this time that the government introduced new incentives for property investors and banks began to loosen their policies for investment loans, freeing up funds for property investing and making the dream of becoming landlords a reality for many. These investors, buoyed with new tax concessions and the ability to own property for a seemingly small weekly outlay, flooded the market with new investments in property, hoping to repeat the success of those before them and aiming to achieve just one thing—large capital gain.

The property market quickly became divorced from other investing as for many the purpose for investing in property appeared to have the single focus of obtaining capital growth for its followers. Over time, many a new scheme has been developed with the aim of achieving this sole objective. We see investors using multiple deposit bonds to buy an abundance of property to sell quickly for gain, amateur renovators buying to 'fix up and sell' and so make a quick profit, and a range of other 'get-rich-quick' schemes where cash flow is irrelevant and capital gain is everything.

Sadly, the '90s delivered to us a gamut of unsuccessful investors who were unable to emulate the success of their predecessors. With an almost unavoidable cooling of property markets nationwide, expected capital gains did not materialise and fully geared investors went to the wall financially as they were unable to support the weekly commitments on their stable of properties. People began to seek out ways to safely invest in property and with the dawn of the new millennium so came a more responsible approach to property investing and a return to the search for cash flow investments.

Today we see a clear division in the strategies of property investors, with growth investors proudly clinging to their ideals in one corner, and cash flow investors espousing their own strategies in the other. Despite dozens of different approaches and many 'tried and true' methods of property investing being taught to the masses by rags-to-riches dynamos via obscenely expensive seminars, there still remains just two objectives for property investors—cash flow today or capital gain tomorrow. Is one more right than the other? Or should the method you ultimately choose for yourself depend on your own financial circumstances and goals for your future? To know just which is right for you, or whether you should be considering a combination of both, let us look at what each type of investor is aiming to achieve.

The method you ultimately choose for yourself should depend on your own financial circumstances and goals for your future

Growth investors

You probably know people who have bought property and made a quick and incredible gain upon sale a few short years later. Although it is most likely that they have not been so lucky with all of their investments and that the true gain is overstated (or stated as a raw figure without considering the actual investment costs), there are people who make a very good living and a great gain out of cleverly choosing the next growth area and buying in low markets to sell in high ones.

The growth investor will typically seek out property that he or she believes has every chance of growing at a greater rate than is the norm. If we said that a 6 per cent per annum growth rate is a conservative average, a growth investor will consistently seek to choose property which performs at well over a 10 per cent per annum growth rate.

Growth investors may use a range of strategies to achieve this. They may seek to buy at below market valuation via a distressed sale or an off-the-plan purchase, selling quickly once the market begins to rise. They may buy and renovate, hoping to add thousands of dollars in value by spending a few hundred dollars and a few hundred hours of their time. They may use specific criteria for second guessing which are the next hot spots, buying a large amount of fully geared property quickly with a view to holding for a set period of time and selling for the gain within that period. Usually growth investors will stick to capital cities where history proves that values will usually rise relatively quickly and usually at a greater rate than regional or country areas. They will seek out areas where demand has begun to outstrip supply and where vacant land is scarce, placing more demand on existing housing and an upward pressure on prices. They will choose well-serviced areas where the population is on the increase, often selecting suburban areas surrounding the major capital cities.

> *The need to obtain property with the greatest potential for capital growth can often mean there is a price to pay*

The need to obtain property with the greatest potential for capital growth can often mean there is a price to pay. As the rent return in capital cities always seems to chase the rising prices, it is usual for weekly rent returns in major centres to sit at somewhere around 0.1% of the purchase price, but it can sometimes be much less. Sudden price booms can mean that relative rent returns fall even lower than this, and it can take some years for the balance to be restored. This means that the investor must be able to fund the shortfall between income and expenses for the term of the investment. While tax breaks can offset this shortfall somewhat, as previously illustrated these high-growth, low-return properties will most likely still result in some weekly cash outlay required by the investor.

Growth investors accept this as the cost of investing, seeing tax benefits as the icing on a cake which is designed to deliver the big payoff in a relatively short period of time. High-income individuals with few personal commitments can often afford to commit large amounts of their income to this strategy and many see the payoff in years to come. As with all investing, there are benefits and drawbacks to this kind of investing.

Benefits for growth investors

❏ The potential to make large gains in a relatively short period of time.

❏ The ability to accumulate assets quickly and so increase net worth.

❏ The potential to get it right, pick the next big boom area and so make a relatively larger profit.

Drawbacks for growth investors

❏ A possible limitation on the number of properties which one investor can buy—equity may increase quickly but without cash flow there will only be so many properties an investor can afford to support.

❏ The chance that the gain will not materialise as expected—resulting in a loss on sale to add to the loss experienced each week.

❏ Possible over-commitment if interest rates suddenly increase.

❐ An inability to liquidate in the event that financial difficulties occur.

❐ An inability to reduce both personal and investment debt in a quicker timeframe.

Cash flow investors

True cash flow investors consider the cash flow of a property above all else. These investors will seek out property which does not cost them money from their own pocket each week—property which actually results in extra money after all is said and done. What these investors do with this extra money is entirely up to them—they may wish to enjoy an enhanced lifestyle today, or use this cash to repay debt more quickly, and so create equity in their property portfolio to enable faster leveraging.

To obtain this kind of cash flow, an investor must find either a property which is positively geared or one which has a positive cash flow after all tax benefits are claimed (see Chapter 1). While there is no rule that says cash flow properties only occur in areas where there is low growth (I personally have high cash flow property in a high growth area in my own portfolio), it is true that cash flow property is more abundant in areas traditionally not expected to experience any sudden or unprecedented booms. This is largely because areas such as these have rent returns which tend to keep pace with the rising prices—and so more of a balance can be seen. Many regional centres close to capital cities and large country towns can see rent returns of 0.13 and 0.14 per cent of the purchase price, effectively closing the gap between income and expenses.

In some cases, many cash flow investors turn to niche market properties to obtain their higher weekly returns. Student accommodation, retirement complexes, and holiday resorts and apartments are all niche market properties which can deliver high returns and excellent on-paper tax deductions. Many of these types of properties can also deliver average or better than average capital gain. However, often the very nature of the investment and the banks' resistance to accepting these types of investments, which can make it difficult to obtain a loan for purchasing, can result in a lower demand for them and so less pressure on prices. This, combined with the fact that niche market properties are often sold at inflated prices to unsuspecting interstate buyers, can result in a slower price increase and so the impression that high cash flow property equals low growth.

Just as a growth investor experiences benefits and drawbacks, so too does a cash flow investor.

Benefits for cash flow investors

❏ The ability to buy more property as usually no personal cash input is required.

❏ No impact on current lifestyle.

❏ The provision of excess funds (the cash flow) which should then be used to eliminate debt and so create equity even if growth does not materialise.

❏ The ability to accumulate a greater number and spread of assets, allowing the liquidation of some to pay down debt leaving the remaining assets to earn an income for retirement.

❏ The provision of a safety net by way of the cash flow— as cash flow investors end up with excess cash each week, they can better manage the risks of vacancy, rising interest rates and lower than expected returns as they have extra cash available to absorb these costs if they occur.

Drawbacks for cash flow investors

❏ If growth is too low, then leveraging will be stalled, or limited to the debt reduction provided by the cash flow.

❏ There can be a difficulty in finding real positive cash flow property that is not just a result of enthusiastic forecasting.

❏ There may be a slower increase in net worth—however, this may be offset by the ability to buy more property than the growth investor who negatively gears if the investor is starting from a high equity base.

How does each method pan out over time?

To consider how each method performs over time, we must make some reasonable assumptions and accept that there will always be an investor somewhere with a different story to tell. No matter how many 'averages' we use, how general the examples shown are, someone will have another example of how it worked quite differently for them. If we can agree that sometimes things happen for apparently no logical reason and know that we can only make assumptions using our best possible (reasonable) guesses based on what we know about history, then we can track an example of each type of investing through to its conclusion and so draw some reasonable assumptions about the outcomes.

The growth investor

Firstly, let's look at a couple who were looking for high capital growth.

Sylvia and Greg had a burning ambition to make fast dollars from high-growth property. They earned a salary of $90,000 ($75,000 for Greg and $15,000 for Sylvia) and had three children. Before investing, they had a net take-home income of $66,413. When they first began to invest five years ago, they came from a very strong position, having paid off their home which was then valued at $400,000. Over a two-year period, they leveraged this equity into eight properties, all located in a capital city but all outside of the period for allowable on-paper deductions. The rent return they saw on these capital city properties was standard (5% for the yearly return or 0.1% a week). These properties also had the following characteristics, as expressed in the opposite table.

Price	Rent (50 wks)	Loan Needed (incl costs)	Loan Cost p.a. (at 6.8%)	Other costs	Raw cost to them
$160,000	$8,000	$170,000	$11,560	$2,500	$6,060
$160,000	$8,000	$170,000	$11,560	$2,500	$6,060
$180,000	$9,000	$190.000	$12,920	$2,300	$6,220
$210,000	$10,500	$220,000	$14,960	$2,000	$6,460
$200,000	$10,000	$210,000	$14,280	$2,500	$6,780
$220,000	$11,000	$230,000	$15,640	$2,000	$6,640
$190,000	$9,500	$200,000	$13,600	$2,500	$6,600
$205,000	$10,250	$215,000	$14,620	$2,500	$6,870
$1,525,000	**$76,250**	**$1,605,000**	**$109,140**	**$18,800**	**$51,690**

From this table, you can see that Sylvia and Greg have raw costs of $51,690 a year from these properties, which in effect gives them a taxable loss of this amount. As Greg was the higher income earner, the properties were all purchased in his name as this was the most tax efficient structure. Therefore, the financial position of Sylvia and Greg is as shown in the table below.

Sylvia		Greg	
Employment income	$15,000	Employment income	$75,000
Property income	$0	Property income	$76,250
Total earned income	$15,000	Total earned income	$151,250
Allowable deductions	$0	Allowable deductions	$127,940
Taxable income	$15,000	Taxable income	$23,310
Tax payable	$1,530	Tax payable	$3,165
Actual earned income	$15,000	Actual earned income	$151,250
Less property costs	$0	Less property costs	$127,940
Less tax	$1,530	Less tax	$3,165
In-hand income	**$13,470**	**In-hand income**	**$20,145**

Now we can see that together Sylvia and Greg realise a net income, after all tax and property costs are considered, of just $33,615— over $32,000 less than they used to receive before they began to invest. It can be said that the commitment made by Sylvia and Greg to this investment strategy is presently costing them $30,000 per annum.

Let's project this forward five years. We will assume that because they have chosen to invest in capital cities they have enjoyed a 10 per cent per annum increase to their portfolio value and now their total portfolio is worth $2,456,000. They decide to sell at this point. During the time they have kept their portfolio, they have paid interest only on their investment loans as their cash flow was so tight.

The results are shown below.

Sale Price	$2,456,000	*minus*
Agents' Commission @ 3.5%	$86,000	*minus*
Outstanding loans	$1,605,000	*minus*
Capital Gains Tax (23.5% on gain minus costs: $765,000)	$179,775	*minus*
Their cash input over 5 years (at $32,798 p.a.)	$163,990	
Actual gain:	**$421,235**	

This is an excellent gain and providing this materialises as hoped this strategy has certainly paid off well for Sylvia and Greg.

It is important to note at this stage, however, that the lifestyle change for Sylvia and Greg to achieve this gain was enormous— in effect, they cut their lifestyle in half and took a gamble that this would pay off over the five-year period. In many cases similar to Sylvia and Greg, this cutback in lifestyle is too much for investors to bear, or they simply cannot make ends meet on the lower household income. For Sylvia and Greg, any liquidation prior to the five-year planned period would have severely dented their profits and greatly lessened the success of this strategy. Add to this the devastation which would most certainly have been felt had there been an unexpected interest rate rise, or a lower than hoped capital gain, and one can see how the prize of the good capital gain has most certainly been paid for with the change in lifestyle and the exposure to quite a large level of risk.

The cash flow investor

Let's now take a look at a different outcome which might be experienced by the cash flow investor.

Naomi and Bill have decided they would like to accumulate property that they can keep forever. They would like to retire in around 12 years' time and feel that they can put together enough property to provide them with a good income in retirement. They too earn $90,000 between them ($66,413 net) but they have their children in private schools and enjoy a range of hobbies, so they cannot afford to cut their current lifestyle spending.

They have made the decision to invest only in positive cash flow property and as such choose a range of property, including a retirement home, student accommodation, resort apartments, and standard residential property from regional areas in NSW, Victoria and WA. Further, they only choose properties that are allowable for on-paper reductions. The property they have chosen has a range of returns, from just 6 per cent through to between 8 and 10 per cent for their niche market property. Across all properties, their cash flow averages $246 a week, and their portfolio encompasses eight properties, like Sylvia and Greg. The characteristics of these properties are shown in the table overleaf.

Price	Rent (50 wks)	Loan Needed (incl costs)	Loan Cost p.a. (at 6.8%)	Other costs	Raw cost to them	Yr 1 Deprec. inc. building
$120,000	$8,250	$130,000	$8,840	$1,600	$2,190	$6,000
$110,000	$6,600	$120,000	$8,160	$1,200	$2,760	$6,800
$180,000	$16,200	$190,000	$12,920	$2,800	$480-	$14,500
$210,000	$18,900	$220,000	$14,960	$2,000	$1,940-	$18,250
$110,000	$8,800	$120,000	$8,160	$1,800	$1,160	$9,200
$125,000	$12,500	$135,000	$9,180	$2,000	$1,320-	$11,500
$190,000	$12,350	$200,000	$13,600	$2,200	$3,450	$9,250
$190,000	$12,350	$200,000	$13,600	$2,200	$3,450	$9,250
$1,235,000	**$95,950**	**$1,315,000**	**$89,420**	**$15,800**	**$9,270**	**$84,750**

> *Note:* Those properties with a high rent return in relation to purchase price
> are niche market properties, which had been purchased with furniture
> included. This furniture, along with the ability to claim a portion of all
> common property including pools, gymnasiums and lifts, is
> responsible for the higher amounts of depreciation allowances.

This example shows that Naomi and Bill have raw costs of $9,270 a year from these properties, which is already a better current position than Sylvia and Greg as not as much pressure is being placed on their lifestyle today. This has been achieved by seeking out those properties with a higher rent return in relation to the purchase price. They too have a taxable loss; however, 'on paper' this has been increased by the depreciation which they can also claim. Remember, depreciation is on-paper only and allows a taxpayer to claim back tax without an associated cost, as it is not an expense. Naomi and Bill have purchased property in Naomi's name only and so she will benefit from the loss, as is shown opposite.

In this example, we can see that together Naomi and Bill realise a net income, after tax and property costs are considered, of $79,200, which is $12,787 more than they were receiving before they started investing! This cash is now available to either enhance their current lifestyle or to repay debt and so create equity more quickly.

Naomi		Bill	
Employment income	$75,000	Employment income	$15,000
Property income	$95,950	Property income	$0
Total earned income	**$170,950**	**Total earned income**	**$15,000**
Allowable deductions	$105,220	Allowable deductions	$0
Allowable depreciation	$84,750	Allowable depreciation	$0
Taxable income	$0	Taxable income	$15,000
Tax payable	$0	Tax payable	$1,530
Actual earned income	$170,950	Actual earned income	$15,000
Less property costs	$105,220	Less property costs	$0
Less tax	$0	Less tax	$1,530
In-hand income	**$65,730**	**In-hand income**	**$13,470**

As it is the aim of Naomi and Bill to keep their properties well into retirement and we can see that this is not costing them anything to do so, it is unlikely that they would wish to sell. In fact, they are in a position to add more properties easily at this stage as they certainly have the cash flow to sustain this. The tax benefits for doing so would be decreased since much of their taxable income has already been offset (and additional properties would most probably be purchased in Bill's name who still has some tax to write-off), but running out of tax breaks should never be a reason to stop buying property if your cash flow and equity allows you to do so.

To draw a comparison to Sylvia and Greg, let's take a look at what the position would be for Naomi and Bill if they did decide to sell after five years. Their choice of niche market property and regional and country areas may well mean they only enjoy a conservative growth across their portfolio. Therefore, let's assume that they have achieved an average of a 6 per cent per annum increase, making the total property values $1,652,700. Due to the cash flow on the properties, they have been able to pay $246 a week over and above the interest repayments into their loan. In reality, this extra cash flow would be increasing every month, as they are reducing debt and so reducing property costs. For the purposes of this illustration, we will keep the repayment at $246 a week over and above the interest bill on fully drawn loans. The results are shown below.

Sale Price:	$1,652,700	*minus*
Agents' Commission @ 3.5%	$57,844	*minus*
Outstanding loans (balance after 5 years)	$1,159,100	*minus*
Capital Gains Tax (23.5% on gain minus costs: $279,856)	$65,766	
Actual gain:	**$369,990**	

This is considerably less than Sylvia and Greg. But let us look at some important points:

❐ Their actual return on purchase price was 29 per cent ($369,990 profit for a $1,235,000 purchase price) while Sylvia and Bill saw 28 per cent ($421,235 profit for a $1,525,000 purchase price).

❐ There is no question that Naomi and Bill will be able to keep their properties for the five-year period as there is not the same strain on their lifestyle as we saw with Sylvia and Greg.

❐ In reality, they may well have added to their portfolio during these five years, as they had both equity and cash flow available for them to do so.

❐ Naomi and Bill had the funds available to manage any economic changes such as interest rate rises or increased vacancy, while Sylvia and Bill would have been forced to sell had any of these things occurred.

❐ There is no reason why Naomi and Bill would actually be unlucky enough across eight properties to see none of these properties perform better than average from a growth point of view. A mere 1 per cent increase in their capital growth (to 7 per cent) would increase their profits by $54,063 and the return on investment to 28 per cent (equal to Sylvia and Greg), while a 1 per cent decrease to Sylvia and Greg's growth would decrease their profits by $109,598, and the return on investment to 21 per cent (less than Naomi and Bill!).

In a sense, the difference between the returns could be said to be the cost of the risk. Sylvia and Greg received a higher return for undertaking a higher amount of risk and discomfort, while Naomi and Bill chose the safer and less painful route which still paid off handsomely for them.

Levelling the playing field

To make the comparison even more fair, we should look at both scenarios and consider that both parties choose to live to the same personal budget. In other words, both parties earn the same from their employment, being $90,000, and spend the same on their lifestyle, being just $33,615. While this will not change things at all for Sylvia and Greg, since their income is already supporting their properties, choosing to slash the personal budget in this way would give Naomi and Bill an extra $630 a week to pay into their loans (including the positive cash flow).

After five years, the balance of their loans would be just $964,659, giving them an extra $269,590 in equity, or cash if they were to sell. This would increase their profits to $564,431, which dramatically increases their return on investment to 45 per cent!

The point I would like to make is that they have the choice. They can either choose to live the same lifestyle as they did before they commenced their portfolio, or choose to make the sacrifices that Sylvia and Greg are forced to make in their chase for capital gain. They have the flexibility to change their approach as their personal circumstances change and they can use cash flow to make up for any capital gain they may lose by choosing against high growth property.

Quite compelling, isn't it? From these examples, we can see that there may be the chance to obtain positive cash flow at the same time that you also access capital gain. I firmly believe it is a myth that cash flow properties are purchased at the cost of capital gain as is asserted by many property investors and advisers alike.

How the myth began

Many years ago, the owners of large hotel chains saw a way to unlock the equity they had in real estate and provide cash flow for their own businesses. By selling off the rooms or apartments (that is the real estate) while retaining the management rights, these operators could continue to make money from what they did best—hotel management—while someone else bore the costs of the actual property, even if it was unoccupied.

The idea had merit, but the difficulty came in pricing the actual real estate for sale. With often very small floor areas, finding suitable property in the same area against which to make a comparison proved almost impossible. The advice of property marketers was sought and based on their wisdom a decision was made to price each property according to its projected return. The following is an illustration of how this worked in practice.

The marketer of a property in a popular seaside resort had studio apartments to sell. These apartments rented for $150 a night, with an average 60% occupancy expected once the operation was underway. This would mean a gross return of $32,850.

This marketer decided that a 7% return would make an attractive proposition without being too enthusiastic and so used this benchmark to place a value on the property, making the price $470,000. This would seem a fair price for a property with such a strong forecast return; however, it ignored the fact that even the best one-bedroom residential apartments opposite the beach were only fetching $400,000.

Cash flow investors seeking to maximise their weekly return flocked to get in on the ground floor of this type of investment, and apartments such as these sold well. One of three outcomes eventuated for these investors:

1   The property traded well and the forecast income was realised. Occupancy was strong, the returns materialised and even when management costs ate into investor profits most still made a positive cash flow if the establishment was successful. Tariffs rose with inflation and resales were successful as strong historical financial records showed that the properties were making money and would most likely continue to do so.

2   The property traded well below forecast, and returns were only 5 per cent, rather than the 7 per cent that had been projected. Since values were linked to returns, this wiped around 40 per cent off the values, creating the rumour that these types of properties actually lost value over time. The fact that they may have been overpriced to begin with was never really considered.

3   The hotel venture failed, leaving investors with no choice but to attempt to find residential occupiers. At best this resulted in a far lower rent return than needed to pay costs and at worst this resulted in investors being left with properties unable to be occupied due to the small size and inappropriateness for owner occupiers.

As the marketers of this type of property often used the 'positive cash flow' angle to market their stock, this abysmal performance played a large role in creating the expectation that any positive cash flow property had little or no chance of obtaining a capital gain over time. Since then, the belief has always been that positive cash flow comes at the cost of capital gain.

There is just as much chance the cash flow investor will see good growth as there is for the growth investor

This, of course, ignores the fact that astute investors today are finding positive cash flow property among standard residential stock all over the country. And, providing the investor is careful to seek out property which satisfies a range of other criteria (to be covered later in this book) as well as having a positive cash flow, there is just as much chance of good growth as there is for the growth investor.

Which one should you choose?

How many times have I wished for a crystal ball? And why can't I have the great benefit of hindsight before the event?

The ideal situation is one where investors receive a good or even great cash flow today, while the value of their overall portfolio increases at an above average rate. All investors should ultimately strive to make this happen and the chances of this can be greatly enhanced if the quality of research done by the investor improves and becomes more efficient.

You must consider each method subjectively, according to how it suits you and your personal financial needs and goals

But, if we were to accept that you had to choose one expected outcome and hope that the other happens as well, you must consider each method subjectively, according to how it suits you and your personal financial needs and goals.

To help you to decide which type of investing strategy you would feel most comfortable with, consider the following profiles of each type of investor.

The growth investor profile

The growth investor:

❑ usually has a set timeframe in which to invest—typically five to ten years, knowing that at the end of this period the portfolio will be liquidated

❑ is not worried about market movements—will stick to the predetermined timeframes despite the economic outlook at any one time

❏ has considerable excess of income after personal expenses and feels that a lifestyle change is a fair price to pay

❏ is comfortable with a higher than average risk factor— with the potential risk mainly linked to poor market timing (getting in while the market is booming and needing to get out at the bottom of a trough)

❏ is prepared to consider a range of growth oriented strategies—for example, buying at distressed sales, buying off the plan, making multiple purchases using deposit bonds, or buying blue chip properties with high price tags and proportionately low rent returns.

The cash flow investor profile

The cash flow investor:

❏ aims to build a portfolio of properties to keep and earn an income from rents after leaving the paid workforce

❏ has limited surplus income and cannot afford to pay money from own pocket

❏ feels uncomfortable with market fluctuations—worries about the impact on interest rates, the issues of vacancy

❏ has a low tolerance to risk—would rather see a lower return if this means cash flow today

❏ is uncomfortable with debt and wishes to have cash flow to assist with the elimination of debt.

Only you can decide which is right for you. Know what you want to achieve in life and what you can manage today. Become familiar with your own risk profile and make decisions which are right for you and your family today, and every day. Only by being firmly in control of your own finances can you make the necessary choices about which strategy suits you best.

Summary

❏ The ultimate investment will provide cash flow today and growth over time.

- ❏ Growth investors are prepared to commit personal funds chasing the capital gain.

- ❏ Cash flow investors will accept lower gains for the safety of the cash flow today.

- ❏ Both methods can work out very well, but a cash flow investor is likely to be able to stay in a distressed market longer due to his or her lack of personal funds commitment.

- ❏ The growth investor will usually have a higher risk profile than the cash flow investor.

- ❏ There is no right or wrong strategy, just ones that are more or less appropriate for an investor's personal circumstances.

Conclusion

Last week a client of mine called while he was away on holidays. He had been procrastinating about investing for about 18 months, but suddenly today was the day he had to make an urgent decision about a property he had seen.

"It's fantastic," he enthused over the telephone. "What makes it so good?" I asked. "It's in a great area!" he said. "How do you know it's great?" I enquired, knowing that he had never been to this area before. "Well it's in a good position," he countered. "For who—you or your tenant?" I said, and so we went back and forth; him stating what he thought were the very important physical reasons why this property was the one for him, and me shooting him down in flames.

Eventually we got down to tin tacks and I asked for the figures. "This property will cost you $80 a week from your own pocket," I told him after working everything out. "That's okay, I guess," he mumbled. Of course it wasn't, as this client was the very person who had spent many months telling me how hard it had been to make ends meet and this was why he was reluctant to invest!

When it came down to it, he was feeling mellow and relaxed (from too much sun I guess) and, since he was having a good time, this led him to make errors in judgement. Once again he, like so many others, fell into the trap of considering the physical appeal of this property (see Chapter 3 for a further discussion of this). My client was looking at the visual aspects over and above the more important things—that is, what his financial goals and tolerance of risk were, and the figures and their ability to help him achieve these financial goals today and in the future.

You must have a strategy—whether you are a growth investor or a cash flow investor, pick your strategy and stick to it. Don't waste time trying to justify why your chosen pathway is better or more profitable than someone else's. Understand that there are many ways in which we can invest, and while most of them may be right, most likely only one will be right for you. And, as I have said many times in the past, the only wrong strategy may well be the one where you choose to do nothing!

3 Shopping for property

- ❐ Buying property in other states is easy if you have a method
- ❐ Say no to negative cash flow
- ❐ Learn about property management to allow you to monitor the efficiency of your manager
- ❐ Complete exhaustive research for every purchase
- ❐ The questions you should ask have nothing to do with physical appeal

If you have read my two previous property books, you will know there is an abundance of tasks for you to complete when you are buying property. Those two books not only covered the best ways to finance your property, but looked at some of the common questions you should be asking before you make the purchase. In addition, the buying process was covered in depth in *How to Create an Income for Life*. Both of these books will provide an invaluable guide to you to help make the purchasing process a little easier.

With the variety of property types now available to the everyday investor, the questions you need to ask are becoming more and more complicated. When you buy property to live in, the questions seem easy—what does it look like, can I put in a pool, will my furniture fit? Investment in property requires a far deeper look into the features which will ensure your property remains profitable for you for many years to come.

Some months ago, I received a letter from an investor who had bought tourism property in Queensland. At first I felt quite sorry for this person, who truly seemed to have had more than his fair share of bad luck. But as I read on it became apparent to me that many of the issues he had could have been avoided altogether had he simply carried out more effective due diligence. The vast majority of his problems sprang from shoddy workmanship by the builder, misleading information from the developer and mismanagement by the on-site manager. Further investigation revealed that all three parties had previously been in some sort of trouble, such as liquidation, formal complaints issued and investigation at one time or another by the Australian Securities and Investments Commission (ASIC)—with all this information being part of public records!

If you are to avoid becoming a party to a failed investment or the subject of a media article, you must know the questions to ask before you sign any contracts or commit to any purchase. You will find some of the more basic questions in *How to Create an Income for Life*. Following are some of the more in-depth and specialised questions that are just as important.

What is the cash flow?

I know I have included cash flow in every book I have ever written and probably in every article, and said it in every interview. By now, you are probably beginning to understand the importance of cash flow! I am committed to positive cash flow investing not just because it has worked for me but because I have witnessed so many other investors facing hardship because their negative cash flow properties were sending them to the wall financially. It's all very well to accept a negative cash flow knowing in your heart that the growth will compensate you eventually. But the cold hard facts are that many, many investors never see these gains as their negative cash flow forces them to liquidate long before it ever materialises.

The very first thing I need to know about a property, even before I ask one single question about the property itself or dare to take a peek at it, is 'what is the cash flow?' This is because I know with absolute conviction that I, like most mere mortals, will easily fall into the trap of becoming emotional about a property once I have laid eyes on it. Hardhearted as I like to think of myself, I too get excited about the physical appeal of any property. I recently took a holiday and stayed in the most gorgeous of apartments, with exceptional 180 degree views of the ocean. The moment I heard that these were for sale, I wanted one. I could see myself letting it out for five years then retiring to simply while away the hours doing what I love most—writing! Even when we discovered that the cash flow was, indeed, negative, my mind tried every trick in the book to convince me that I could accept the negative because the property was so good. Fortunately, I have a very commercially minded husband who refused to listen to my skewed reasoning and now that I am back on terra firma I can appreciate his wisdom and see what a doomed investment it would have been!

> If the cash flow is not positive, you must move on

If the cash flow is not positive, you must move on. Say no. There is nothing about that property that can make up for the fact that you will be out of pocket every week and that your continued investing will be negatively impacted if you run out of funds to support your properties. Later in this chapter you will find some reference material that will allow you to make quick assumptions about on-paper costs so you can have a fair idea if the cash flow will be positive or not before you move any further down the track with a particular property.

Do the cash flows last?

It could be that you have found a great investment and the cash flows look great. But will they last? As you will see once you have read Chapter 5, depreciation of fixtures, fittings and furniture can experience a very large decline after year one, depending on the method of depreciation you ultimately choose. This is due to the combined effects of both the decreasing value upon which you are able to claim depreciation and that in year one a property can often have low-value items which are accepted for a 100 per cent write-off—and once written off there is no more claim to make. If the property you are considering has a low positive cash flow in year one, it may be that this low cash flow will be wiped out in subsequent years.

In order to better manage your entire portfolio, you must carry out projections beyond year one when making your choice for purchase. While this can be a very hard task where a depreciation schedule is unavailable, many new properties do come with sample reports that you can use to calculate some quick figures.

> Sara was buying property with: a rent return of $10,000 a year, interest on the loan of $11,500 a year, expenses of $2,000 and total depreciation of $22,000. In year one, she would be able to use $8,800 of this depreciation and as she was in the 47% tax bracket this meant that she would see a positive cash flow on this property of $43 a week. In year two, however, her depreciation claim fell to only $3,000. This year, this property will actually cost Sara $8.55 a week.

However, calculating raw figures such as this will not tell the whole story. Sara may well have used the positive cash flow and debt reduction strategies to reduce her debt and so the property costs. In doing so, she may be able to keep this property positive every year, even as her deductions begin to run out. In addition, over the years Sara should see a rental increase and so an increase to her income. As her deductions reduce, her costs should also reduce (through interest reduction on her loan) and her income should increase. The gap between income and expenses will gradually close and she will no longer need the on-paper deductions to provide her positive cash flow.

When you begin to look for positive cash flow property you must look beyond the first year and make some attempts to ascertain the likely long-term outcome for you. Will you be able to use the positive cash flow and perhaps some of your own excess personal funds to reduce debt? Are most of the on-paper deductions used up in year one? Considering your portfolio as a whole and your expectation of adding more property as and when your equity allows, does the overall cash flow remain positive across all of your property? This is where the work comes in; however, once you become proficient at these calculations you will easily be able to master the skills of efficient cash flow purchasing.

When you begin to look for positive cash flow property you must look beyond the first year

What must I know about the property management?

To be able to choose effectively and supervise the right property manager, you must almost become a 'manager of property managers'. This does not mean that you don't hand over the management task to the manager you are paying—rather it means that you must have a clear understanding of the job you intend for him or her to do. If the property you are considering is standard residential, be very sure that you know everything there is to know about the costs of property management in the state in which you are looking. Property management costs can vary greatly from state to state, and even from manager to manager. If the positive cash flow is small to begin with, sometimes the added costs of inspections, letting fees, advertising costs and sundries can push this positive cash flow into a negative, especially when you add periods of vacancy to the equation. In addition to the figures, you must try to find out more about the property managers themselves. More information about having your property managed can be found in Chapter 7.

If you are looking at property with some kind of on-site manager, your task becomes far more complex and there are many more things you must know. I am alarmed at how little research people undertake into the entity which is ultimately going to be responsible for the success (or failure) of their investment!

Before you proceed with any investment requiring external management, the following questions will give you the absolute minimum information you will need.

What is the nature of management?

Is the management a 'management rights' arrangement, where an entity has purchased the rights of management (making it far harder to terminate them in the event that mismanagement occurs) or is it a 'management agreement', where on-site management is provided by way of a contract between the owners (as a body corporate) and the manager. This type of agreement may be easier to terminate should the need arise.

What is the true cost of management?

You need to work out the true cost of management as a percentage of return, as all too often this is not fully disclosed before you sign on the dotted line. While the management fee itself may be seven or eight per cent of return (as an example only), often the associated costs of management—such as pool chemicals, cleaning, linen and laundry, telephone charges and other sundries —can severely blow out the final cost to the owner. I have seen managed complexes where the final figure of the management charges was an astounding 50 per cent of the gross return. Again, this may be acceptable if the return is very high but you must know about these things beforehand.

What is the experience of the manager?

Management rights are commonly purchased by couples who are seeking a lifestyle change. Many times the manager has no past experience whatsoever and so must rely on either the processes of the previous (possibly unsuccessful) manager or on new processes with which he or she is not familiar. Where the manager is a large organisation, find out about its other projects by asking to see annual reports and other documentation relating to the outcomes it has previously been able to achieve. Don't fall into the trap of relying on the experience of the manager just because it has a name you know well—many big name hotel operators have experienced financial difficulty relating to mismanagement and there are also cases where the large name operator subleases the management rights to a smaller, less experienced one.

What is the commercial background of the operator?

To see if the operators have experienced any prior financial difficulties such as receivership or bankruptcy, you should do a background check on them. Much of this information is a part of public record. Be sure to find out what other past or current companies the operators have been involved in so that you can also check out those companies.

Does the operator have a business plan?

The failure of many businesses can largely be attributed to their lack of planning. The entity responsible for earning an income for you must have a clearly laid out business plan and you should have access to this.

What are the terms of any rent guarantee?

You should be aware that most rent guarantees consist of a 'promise' to deliver a certain level of income with little or no financial backing. Under these circumstances, should occupancy not reach desired levels the rent guarantee cannot be delivered and rarely is the operator under any legal obligation to do so. Sometimes the rent guarantee is provided by using some of the purchase price of each property to provide a pool of funds to top up rent in periods of low occupancy. This means that you have simply paid more for your property than it is worth for the guarantee of having cash flow and this may not be a worthwhile exercise.

Is there a leaseback?

A leaseback is where your property is actually leased by the operators or managers, so they are paying your rent to you whether there is a tenant or not. Where a leaseback has been provided, you need to check what the financial status of the entity providing this leaseback is. This is because, while a leaseback can be reassuring for an owner, if the operators' only access to funds is through the renting of your property, they will be unable to honour this lease if they experience high vacancy. Some operators derive income from other sources, such as through the operation of a restaurant or bar, and this can be used to fund leasebacks if necessary.

A management agreement is not an automatic recipe for success

Always remember that any type of management is not an automatic recipe for success. Your responsibilities are not dissolved simply because the management of your new property is already in place.

Who are the developers?

Where the property you are looking at is new or is being purchased off the plan, try to find out as much as you can about the developers prior to proceeding. It is highly likely that they have completed other projects and you must know how successful they have been. Try to ascertain who the developers are using to carry out the actual building and explore the quality of their work on other buildings. Investigate the financial history of both the developers and the builders and be sure that you know about prior or other companies in which they have been involved. There exists many a developer and builder fresh from bankruptcy who manage to start new companies. It would be useful to know about their backgrounds and, if there are past problems, the reasons for them occurring. If you discover a string of unhappy purchasers in their pasts, this could be cause for concern.

How happy and healthy is the body corporate?

A poorly managed body corporate can spell future problems. Where a body corporate becomes illiquid due to its inability to properly plan for future expenditure, individual owners can often be called upon to make additional contributions via a special levy to manage any structural problems or other common property repair work and these can be very costly. Unexpected expenses play havoc with cash flow and can turn a previously profitable investment into a money pit.

It is possible in many states to institute a Body Corporate search. This will uncover any undisclosed financial difficulties and also expose any legal action that may have been taken against bodies corporate for past actions.

What are council's plans for the area?

You may have found the perfect three-bedroom townhouse in a market where demand for three-bedroom townhouses is quite pronounced. However, what you may not know is that 20 other development applications for three-bedroom townhouse complexes are already in council and approved. This, of course, may impact negatively on your ability to attract a tenant in the future, especially if the population growth is low or static. Be sure you are familiar with what is planned for the area in which you want to invest. If a rock stadium or new airport is planned for next door, you may experience future difficulties with finding a tenant, not to mention a possible negative impact on values. In addition to the searches commonly carried out by most conveyancers, take some time to do some of your own research to uncover any of these little surprises which may have some effect on the viability of your investment.

Does this niche market property have a dual purpose?

Niche market property is any property that has been built with a specific end use in mind. The category comprises hotel and other tourist accommodation, seniors homes and retirement villages, student accommodation, and other such specialist market properties. Property such as this can be an important part of your portfolio. It can provide a good cash flow and better than average capital gain where the venture has been a success. If you have purchased a tourism property, for example, which is always heavily booked and delivers a nice cash flow income, it is highly likely this property will not only be highly liquid but it will grow quickly in value as well, as tariffs are raised with inflation and investor demand grows.

However the reverse can sometimes be true—the developer just didn't get it right and you are left with a property with high vacancy which you are also unable to offload to someone else without taking a huge loss.

You can somewhat decrease the risk of being caught with a property unable to be occupied or sold if you make sure that the property is one suited to another purpose and not simply designed for a single end use.

For example, many properties built close to universities for the student market have been designed expressly for student needs— these properties may have four to five bedrooms, each with a bathroom, and a large common room area. In the event that these are no longer viable for students or the demand falls below supply, it would be difficult to re-let these properties to the standard residential market due to their cumbersome design. The same could be said for small hotel rooms or holiday apartment accommodation with total areas of less than 50 square metres— these would be difficult to market as owner-occupied residences and, should the tourism market not sustain an income for the owners, they may be left with a bit of a white elephant.

Be sure that any niche market property you choose is easily convertable into an owner-occupier residence. It must have adequate living areas, be close to services and provide all of the basic features that a tenant will seek. Properties such as these are also far more likely to be attractive to your bank and lending difficulties may then not apply.

Is there perpetual demand for rental accommodation?

Although this question harks back once again to the need to have a crystal ball, there are some simple questions you can ask which will help you to maximise the chances of success in finding continued tenants for the property you are considering buying. They include:

❐ What has the population growth been like in the past few years in the area you are considering buying a property— is it growing, stable or going backward?

❐ What is the economy of the area like? High inflation and low job vacancies mean that there are not enough jobs in the area for the population. This will lead to the working population moving away from the area, a gradual decline in the efficiency of the economy and a weakening of commerce. This eventually results in a decreasing population.

❐ What is the availability of land in the area? An abundance of land in an area with an increasing population combined with the availability of government incentives for home buyers and an increase in competition between builders will mean that more people have the opportunity to own their own home, which will reduce the depth of the tenancy market. Where land is scarce but the economy is strong and population is increasing, more people will rent and there will be an upward pressure on prices as demand for property outstrips supply.

❐ What is the availability of services in the area—for example, shopping centres, schools and transport—and are there planned improvements to these to continue to foster the growth in population? Poor planning on the part of local and state governments can stall the growth of an area.

❐ If the area you are looking to buy in is a regional one, what is its proximity to a large city? People will and do commute as much as two hours each way to work, and due to the recent overheating of capital city markets there are many regional areas outside of capital cities which are about to experience great demand both from a tenancy and a purchasing point of view.

What is the age of the property?

Older properties can provide a positive cash flow in the form of positive gearing. Usually this type of property will be found in country areas with a strong industrial infrastructure and they offer the opportunity to buy low-cost property with strong rental returns. The main problems with older properties are that not only are they ineligible for on-paper deductions but you can expect that you may begin to experience some of the problems which are part of the territory with older properties. Among the commonly occurring problems are hot water service breakdowns, structural problems, termites, and wall and ceiling cracks just to name a few. All of these spell money and can be just the start of a range of problems.

I like to buy property that is up to 10 years old, 15 at the most. Providing it is sturdily built, I should see many years before I need to make any major repairs and I can also access on-paper deductions which can further enhance my cash flows.

What is the demand for property like this?

You must know whether or not there is going to be a tenant for your property once it has settled. If you ask the selling agents, they will reassure you that, yes, of course, there is much demand. The truth is, they probably don't know and it is an easy little fib to get away with—after you settle, if you cannot get a tenant the agent will simply tell you that the market has taken a sudden and unsuspected turn.

Here is where you can earn points for being a little crafty. Find a property manager from another real estate agent in the same area as you would like to buy and call him, pretending you are a potential tenant. Tell him you wish to lease a property, outlining your needs (of course, describing the property you are considering buying) and ask him what is available. If he comes back with dozens of choices, you will know that supply is greater than demand. If he tells you there is not much around, bingo! You may be onto something.

Am I being commercial in my approach?

Those who know me will be able to recognise when I adopt my soap box approach. This is where I hound investors to become absolutely clinical in their approach to property. This is easier said than done, of course. The reason I am so clever about being unemotional is that I cannot count how many times I have wanted to buy property because I unconsciously had visions of myself living there one day (you have no idea how many potential beachside suburbs I have pictured myself living in!).

> *Look at the facts in the cold hard light of day and totally divorce yourself from any emotional attachment to a potential purchase*

If you know you will not be able to look at the facts in the cold hard light of day and totally divorce yourself from any emotional attachment to a potential purchase, get someone else to find the property for you. You will not possibly be able to think commercially about any purchase if you start to feel warm and fuzzy every time you think about the property. If you know this is you, do what I did with my last purchase—buy it off the internet!

When I tell people how I did this, I hear horrified gasps and witness their amazement that I could possibly consider such a move. This confuses me—why not purchase off the internet? If I have asked all of the required questions, if I know there is a deep tenant market and a demand for this property, if I know the age, the size, the number of bedrooms, the management arrangements and every other little detail, what possible difference could its actual appearance make to its effectiveness as an investment?

Have you ever been to a trash and treasure market, marvelled at some of the absolute rubbish for sale and then marvelled some more when you see someone actually purchasing some of that rubbish? They say one man's trash is another's treasure, and the same could be said for property. You may look at a property and hate it, while someone else thinks it is the latest thing in nouveau chic! So, looking at a property and feeling good about its appearance is not going to change its effectiveness as an investment.

Assessing the cash flows before you buy

The question I am asked most commonly is, "How can I know what a property will provide in on-paper deductions before I buy it?" Of course, the straight answer to this is you can't, unless you are buying a new property which comes with a sample depreciation schedule. Even in this situation, you can't always rely on these samples to be accurate and I have seen some sample reports which do appear to stretch the rules just a little too far.

When I look at potential property, my experience helps me to make assumptions about the property without the need to pay a quantity surveyor to prepare a report which I may not use. In order to make your own search a little easier, I have reproduced the following ready reckoner which gives some 'rule of thumb' examples of the kind of depreciation you may find in the property you are looking at (see opposite). Note that the depreciation amounts supplied include both the special building write-off and the depreciation on fixtures, fittings and furniture, and are based on the diminishing value method (see Chapter 5). Also note that this ready reckoner applies to new buildings. Established buildings should have an adjustment made for lower construction costs and lower values on the fixtures and fittings—say, 5 per cent for each year of age.

From this table, you can see that if we assumed a purchase of a house at the price of $250,000, a loan for $260,000 at 6.8 per cent ($17,680 in interest payments) and additional costs each year of $2,000, an investor in the 47 per cent tax bracket would need to see at least $300 a week return in order for this purchase to provide a positive cash flow (after he receives his tax benefits). This amount has been calculated by ascertaining the minimum amount needed to cover all costs after considering the tax breaks. An investor purchasing a unit for $300,000 would need to see $320 a week in order to achieve the positive cash flow.

Building Type	$ Purchase Price	$ Year 1 Depreciation	$ Year 1–5 Total Depr.
1 BR Unit	300,000	8,000	38,000
2 BR Unit	400,000	10,000	50,000
3 BR Unit	450,000	12,000	60,000
Townhouse	300,000	5,000	25,000
Townhouse	400,000	6,500	30,000
House	250,000	4,800	24,000
House	375,000	6,250	28,000

Reproduced here with the permission of BMT and Associates, Quantity Surveyors.

This is not to say that units always provide greater on-paper deductions than houses and are therefore a better investment. While a unit can provide greater on-paper deductions if there are many common property deductions, there may be other trade-offs over the longer term, such as greater illiquidity or lower growth. Each individual property must be considered on its individual merits and no two properties are likely to provide the same tax benefits.

Do be aware that where an actual schedule is unavailable and your calculated cash flow is very low after using this ready reckoner you will have little room to move and you may end up with a negative cash flow property once you have a report prepared. Where the cash flow is very high, then any differences in the final figure may not have such a big impact. Be sure to use this reckoner as a guide only and remember that it may not be accurate at all for the property you ultimately buy.

Summary

☐   The first question you ever ask should be about the cash flow—this will eliminate non-starters and save you a lot of time inspecting or researching properties that were never going to work for you.

☐   Be sure the cash flows will last for more than just the first year.

☐   Become familiar with your property manager and be sure to give the task of choosing one the requisite amount of consideration.

☐   Where management agreements or management rights are involved, added due diligence is a must. Most failed niche market property investment occurs when investors are careless in this area.

☐   Know the background of your developer and carry out complete checks of his or her credentials.

☐   Look for skeletons in the closet of the body corporate— you may end up literally paying for any of their past mistakes.

☐   Be sure the council does not plan to oversupply the market in the area in which you are looking to buy.

☐   Try to know ahead of time if demand for the kind of accommodation you are considering is on the increase or the decline.

☐   At all times, maintain a commercial approach to the transaction.

Conclusion

All too often I receive enthusiastic phone calls from clients, often made from their mobile phones while they stand inside a property they have fallen in love with, to ask me if I think the purchase is a 'good idea'. This is like asking if a property is in a 'good area'— usually the interpretation of 'good' by the purchaser has nothing to do with the actual investment potential. To buy property which you feel 'good' about is ignoring the very real need to diligently research your market in a wide range of areas.

Knowing the answers to the questions discussed in this chapter, along with those questions outlined in my last book, should put you in pretty good stead to make a purchasing decision. While you can never take the risk completely out of property investing and while there is no such thing as an iron-clad guarantee, you will have eliminated some of the more obvious issues which could arise for the careless investor and so given yourself the best possible chance of success. Be sure the questions you ask are asked of the right people. The developer or vendor's agent will only tell you what he or she needs to tell you to effect a sale. Be clear about what you want and smart about how you get the answers to your questions and you will be well on your way to a profitable and efficient investing future.

4 Managing your portfolio

- [ ] Your property portfolio may contain a wide range of different kinds of property
- [ ] Niche market property can play an important role in all portfolios

In my perfect investing world, everybody takes my advice, successfully buys dozens of highly positive cash flow properties, and we all meet every year on a yacht in the Whitsunday Islands to celebrate how much more clever we were than the rest of the country! The future holds a veritable nation of wealthy retirees who all toast their own brilliance as they attend social gatherings of like-minded people and spend their hoards of cash travelling the world and being given their own personal shopping assistant at Harrods.

In the real world, this will never happen. While positive cash flow property is marvellous, it's just not that abundant. In some cases, positive cash flow property may provide great benefits in year one and fizzle badly in year two, long before you get the chance to minimise your debt and so reduce your costs. And what about all of those people who already have a stable of negative cash flow properties? Just where do they turn from here?

Being realistic, we must consider what any one person can feasibly achieve. We need to take into account not only the availability of positive cash flow property but also the fact that sometimes people may still choose property with negative cash flow, for whatever reason. We must also know that many niche market properties, while providing highly positive cash flow, can bring with them a host of other problems, such as management issues as well as funding difficulties. It is in this chapter that I would like to explore all of these issues, and perhaps provide some strategies for minimising the impact of anything negative which may arise in your own portfolio.

What is the norm?

Of course, there is no quick answer to this question. I have clients with seven or eight good cash flow properties, while others have many negative cash flow ones. Still others have stumbled along, selecting property using their emotions and finding themselves with a mix of positive and negative cash flow properties.

I think my own property portfolio is probably a pretty good example of what a cash flow investor may have after a few years. This is what I have at the time of writing:

❑ An owner-occupied home (no income but lots of equity), which has seen a doubling of its value in five years.

❑ Two flats by the beach at a holiday destination—cash flow is great in a good year, equalling around $70 a week. However, after three years only two have been positive due to a downturn in travellers after September 11 and the Ansett collapse. The trade-off has been an exceptional but unexpected growth, with the value almost tripling in three and a half years.

❑ A two-bedroom unit in far-north Queensland. Positive cash flow in years one and two, even cash flow in three and negative cash flow in four due to the need for me to drop the rent for six months when vacancy rates grew. This year it is back to even. We have seen no capital growth in this property—probably because we were typical 'Southern States' purchasers caught by two-tier marketing who paid too much in the first place. For almost six years we have been told to expect a boom and this finally appears near.

❏ A house in the suburbs of a capital city. This property appeared to have a raw negative cash flow, but is now $10 a week positive cash flow after having had a quantity surveyor's report prepared. It is built on a large dual occupancy block and we have since built a second dwelling. Great tenants, quite a young property and the least of my worries.

❏ Three flats in the country. Very old so no on-paper deductions, but highly cash flow positive (positively geared) with interest on the loan at $6,500 a year and rent return $15,000 when fully occupied. High turnover of tenants but the cash flow manages this well. Not a great chance of growth at this stage although they are near a major regional centre which is experiencing a boom, so you never know.

❏ A large commercial office space—my first commercial property.

As you can see, I have a pretty good spread of property types, and the aim of all of them upon purchase was to obtain a positive cash flow. Until recently, all of the investment loans remained fully drawn and I paid interest only, using the cash flow to pay off the debt on my own home, which has now been finalised. I also have considerable investment in shares and international initial public offerings as well as a large financial investment into Destiny Financial Solutions.

The original value of this property portfolio, if you consider each of the purchase prices, was $1,350,000, with three of the properties having only been purchased recently. The value today of the entire portfolio is $2,500,000, which is a flat 85 per cent increase (provided by the five properties that were the only ones I owned until recently), or almost 11 per cent compounding per annum as an average. I have managed to eliminate a good chunk of the debt of the portfolio, having concentrated on the personal portion of this debt. I started this portfolio with around $100,000 in cash, which I used to pay the deposit and costs on the owner-occupied property. The rest have been fully geared and I have leveraged as the equity grows.

No doubt many readers would have achieved far more than this, and some of you may be thinking that it is you who should be writing books! However, I have bought property within the parameters of my own risk tolerance and it has been successful for me. While I was extremely conservative in the beginning, I have become a little more aggressive as I buy more and increase my net worth, and so decrease my exposure to risk. If I needed to today, I could sell all of my investments and still own my own home outright, and this is comfortable for me. This was not the case when I began and it is a good demonstration of how it takes only a short while to reach that point where the security factor has increased enough to make the level of real risk very low.

Spread your investing and concentrate on obtaining good cash flow

My own portfolio is a great example, I believe, of how if you spread your investing and concentrate on obtaining good cash flow, you most probably will also obtain some good performers and so good growth somewhere in your portfolio.

Your own portfolio

If you have already commenced your property portfolio, chances are you will have many questions about what to do next. Every day I answer dozens of queries from people at various stages of their investing, the main themes of which have been summarised in the sample questions in Chapter 8. Following are some of the more common issues that have been raised, and my suggestions for managing them.

Help! I think I have bought a lemon!

How do you know if you have actually bought a lemon? Sometimes it is clear—no one will rent it or the returns are far below what the developer's agent told you they would be. In the latter instance, while you may have a case for misleading and deceptive conduct, this can be hard to prove and basically there are few laws which can really protect us against developers who overstate projected incomes.

Basically a lemon will be any property which:

❒ has more than eight weeks a year vacancy for standard residential, or less occupancy than you need to pay your costs for niche market property—I mention this because some niche market property can provide a positive cash flow even at 30 per cent occupancy if the deductions and returns are high

❒ goes backwards in value and has a low cash flow

❒ has a negative cash flow and an average or below average growth rate

❒ is in a less secure area and so is always being vandalised by the tenants or others, meaning it costs you more money in repair bills than it gives you in income.

Don't fall into the trap of believing that just because a property has little or even no growth and a low cash flow that it is a lemon (take my far-north Queensland property, as an example). It is perfectly acceptable to have a plodder like this in your portfolio, although you are probably making it hard for yourself if all of the properties in your portfolio are like this.

If you own property with some of the above characteristics and believe that it may well be a lemon, I would suggest the following:

❒ If the impact on you today is that you are not able to make ends meet because your investment property is a money pit, you must sell now. Don't make the mistake of hanging onto it hoping for that elusive capital gain or because you believe that you have to try to recoup your losses. Although property markets do go in cycles, these cycles are measured and expressed as an average only. This means that within these cycles, a property in any one area can still stay in a trough indefinitely and behave very differently to the average. You could grow old and die before that gain finally comes, and meanwhile you have led a dismal existence, feeding money perpetually into a loss making venture.

Sell the property, cut your losses (remembering that a capital loss can be carried forward to future years to offset capital gains), but be sure to go right back in and invest again. The country is full of people who bought one property, sold it within five years and never bought again, having made no improvement in their financial circumstances.

❐ If the property is going backwards but still has a positive cash flow, I would be inclined to hang onto it unless the slide is remarkable, which is unlikely. In truth, the only reason a property ever really goes backwards is if you paid too much in the first place. It is more likely that the property will remain static for some time and this is okay if occupancy remains good. It is acceptable to have a property in your portfolio that does not perform from a growth point of view, as long as this does not apply to every property you buy. If it is your only investment, be sure to double your efforts at debt elimination on a property such as this so you can still create equity and leverage again.

❐ If the property has a negative cash flow and obvious signs of distress from a growth point of view (tumbleweeds in the main street are a sure sign that a ghost town is imminent) then you may be best to sell now and get straight back into the market with a more suitable cash flow property, particularly if the cash flow is hurting your budget as well.

❐ If you have a property which attracts unsavoury tenants and you have used up all the favours offered by your landlord's insurer, this may again be a good reason to sell and cut your losses. Investing needs to be fun, not a major headache and you do not need this kind of hassle in your life.

A client of mine recently purchased a negatively geared property (yes, even my personal clients ignore me from time to time!), assuring me that this was okay because the positive cash flow on his first purchase (made some months before) could pay the negative cash flow on the second. This is an interesting approach and may be one which pays off if the negatively geared property has clear signs that it has other features which spell profits or leveraging power to you. But please, don't let a nicely positive cash flow property give you the excuse to buy a negative cash flow property which you like for purely emotional reasons. Remember my motto—use your head, not your heart.

What do I do when I get to retirement?

Many people have asked me what their ultimate exit strategy should be. Personally, I think that while it is important to have a goal, we should

As our personal circumstances change, so will our goals

also realise that as our personal circumstances change so will our goals. Becoming too hooked up with a particular exit strategy may cause you to miss some good opportunities along the way. Ideally, the perfect exit strategy would look something like the following two examples.

Rajan bought 18 properties over a 15-year period. By the time he reached retirement his properties were worth $4.2m and he owed $1.7m on them. He sold enough properties to pay off the debt and give him some cash in the bank ($100,000) and kept the remaining properties to provide him an income. If we presumed just 5% average return on these properties, this gave Rajan an income of $120,000 per annum.

Chelsea bought 12 properties in 12 years. Her portfolio was valued at $2.9 m and she owed $1.3m. As she no longer wanted the responsibility of being a landlord, she sold all of her properties, realising $1.6m which she then invested in a range of managed funds and pension plans. She chose to receive an income of $70,000, reinvesting the rest as part of these plans.

Note: Capital gains tax and selling costs would, in reality, apply and change the ultimate yearly incomes received by both Rajan and Chelsea.

Either way, the efforts these people made during their lifetimes resulted in choice for them upon retirement. Neither of these two would qualify for any government pension or benefits, and both would continue to pay tax—but so what? I certainly hope to remain in a tax paying, independent position for the rest of my life!

The point is, once retirement presents itself the choice will be yours. It may be that you do not wish to sell at all. In Rajan's case, leaving the paid workforce would probably have very little impact on his income, as most of it comes passively from his investments. As rental income can be the only form of unearned income that most banks will accept for lending purposes (income from shares and managed funds is usually not accepted), there is no reason that Rajan cannot keep his entire portfolio and even continue to add to it! In doing so, Rajan will continue to use other people's money (namely, the bank's) to gain access to the rising market that property usually presents, further increasing his net worth every year.

What is the value of the property portfolio I will need?

This is a question that continues to baffle people. Further, seminar presenters who use frightening statistics and visions of old people starving in the streets to try to scare us into submission and sell their property to us when we are at our most vulnerable do little to answer it. If you consider that the average pension today is $18,000 per couple and the average investment of a retired person adds around $5,000 to this income, you will only need to accumulate enough property to produce an income of $23,000 a year (all calculated in today's terms) to be in a better position than most of the retired population. In simple terms, this means that your own goal could be to accumulate income producing property resulting in just $460,000 net worth (not including your family home, which, of course, is not a financial asset).

Look at how easy this can be. Let us assume that you have a home worth $250,000 in which you have $150,000 equity (that is, you owe $100,000), and a ten-year period in which you would like to invest. Let us also assume, once again, a very conservative capital growth rate of 6 per cent and that despite accessing positive cash flow property you use this cash flow at the hairdressers or the club (shame on you) rather than ploughing it back into the mortgages. You would like to keep an element of safety in your investing, so you choose never to borrow more than 80 per cent of your total equity. What could happen if you invest under these circumstances is demonstrated in the following diagrams.

In year one, you buy three properties valued at $125,000 each, with $7,500 in purchasing costs each, making the total loan required for each $132,500. Using the property you live in for security alongside the new ones you are buying, your debt will look like the diagram below.

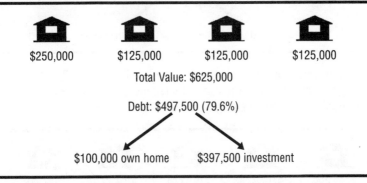

$250,000 $125,000 $125,000 $125,000

Total Value: $625,000

Debt: $497,500 (79.6%)

$100,000 own home $397,500 investment

After one year, your total portfolio has grown to $662,500, and we will assume that you have not paid anything off the principal of your debt at all (although this is unlikely). You have created enough equity to add another similarly priced property to your mix and now your situation is as shown below.

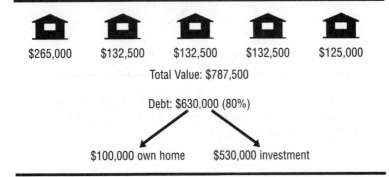

$265,000 $132,500 $132,500 $132,500 $125,000

Total Value: $787,500

Debt: $630,000 (80%)

$100,000 own home $530,000 investment

Two more years pass, and you are now in year four. Your portfolio, having grown at 6 per cent each year, is worth $884,835. You owe $630,000, so can afford to add two more properties to your mix, as shown below.

$297,754 $148,877 $148,877 $148,877 $140,450 $125,000 $125,000

Total Value: $1,134,835

Debt: $895,000 (78.8%)

$100,000 own home $795,000 investment

In year six, your total portfolio is now worth $1,275,100 and you owe $895,000. You can add three more properties this year as shown in the diagram below.

$334,556 $167,278 $167,278 $167,278 $157,809

$140,450 $140,450 $125,000 $125,000 $125,000

Total Value: $1,650,099

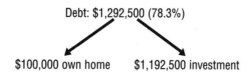

Debt: $1,292,500 (78.3%)

$100,000 own home $1,192,500 investment

In year eight, your properties are now worth $1,854,041 and you owe $1,292,500. You can add five more properties to your portfolio, as shown opposite.

$375,907 $187,953 $187,953 $187,953 $177,314

$157,809 $157,809 $140,450, $140,450 $140,450

$125,000 $125,000 $125,000 $125,000 $125,000

Total Value: $2,479,048

Debt: $1,955,000 (78.8%)

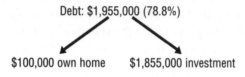

$100,000 own home $1,855,000 investment

In year ten, your properties are now worth $2,952,585. Your own home is valued at $447,711, meaning you have $2,504,873 worth of investment property. You sell this property to repay all of your debt, leaving you with a lump sum of $549,873, which if invested at just 5 per cent would give you $27,493 a year and $38,491 if you could access a 7 per cent return.

Of course, over a ten-year period you would not always be able to buy property for just $125,000, as the price of even the lowest end property will rise over this period. But all things are relative and as the prices rise so does the amount by which the properties appreciate each year. In addition to this, a more likely scenario would be that, at the very least, the family home would be paid off in full (adding $100,000, or $5,000 a year to the income) and some of the cash flow may have been used to further reduce debt. Add to that the fact that in any ten-year cycle there are likely to be some higher than average growth rates and $27,000 becomes the absolute least a person would expect as an income from this strategy, with much higher incomes the greater likelihood. My experience with my clients is that most people can comfortably achieve a $1,000,000 net worth in a ten-year period—resulting in a $50,000 per annum income if invested with a 5 per cent return—with hard work, astute investing and, most importantly, diligent debt elimination.

Should I sell a property after the big capital gain has occurred?

Ah, the $64,000 question at last! You have been lucky enough to buy a property just before a boom and while the gains have been enormous, they appear to have slowed down—so what should you do?

I had this very thing happen to me six years ago. I bought a property with my parents, for them to live in. I rarely refer to this property, since it was not income producing for me and the profits have been used to build an extension onto my home for my parents to live in. We paid $190,000 for this property and sold it four years later when they decided to move on for $325,000. At the time, many people asked me why I didn't buy the other half off my parents, since the gain had been so good during the four years and the property appeared to qualify as 'blue chip' property.

The main reason was, had I chosen to rent out the property when it was bought for $190,000 it would have been positive cash flow, as it would have attracted a rent return of around $280 a week. However, if I needed to raise the funds to buy the other half at the new valuation of $325,000, this property most certainly would not have been positive cash flow given that the rental returns had barely moved.

The other reason was that I truly felt the big gains had come and gone, at least for the next ten years or so anyway. Such a huge rise could not be sustained, and the reasons for this rise, which included an improvement to the infrastructure in the area, were now in the past with nothing new or notable on the horizon.

Had I bought this property alone in the first place and with the goal to make an income, I certainly would have kept it as the vastly increased equity could have been leveraged into more property without having to sell that one. If, on the other hand, I was fully committed in the eyes of the bank and could not access additional borrowings, keeping this property, which may have already had its heyday, may have held me back from accessing other property with a positive cash flow. Under these circumstances, I would consider selling—taking the profits and using them to buy more property that had all the characteristics necessary for successful investing.

How much should I spend on each property?

How much you spend on your investment properties depends on how much you have to begin with or how much equity you have in property you already hold. The truth is many people are probably in a position to invest without realising this to be the case. The problem is that these days most of the advertisements for investment properties offer opportunities to invest that cost many hundreds of thousands of dollars, and so a message is

Many people are probably in a position to invest without realising this to be the case

being sent that investing in property is, by its very nature, an expensive exercise. People have been led to believe that for success in property investing one needs to purchase high end, blue chip property.

One of my clients has four properties, and not one of them has cost any more than $70,000! She first thought about investing four years ago but could never bring herself to do so. She had many false starts, always getting to the stage where she had to sign a contract before suddenly pulling out. She had a real sense of not wanting to overcommit herself, and was worried she would lose her house. Despite me carefully explaining to her how unlikely this event would be, I just could not get her over the line. After thinking about this long and hard, I started to encourage her to research the properties I had seen that had prices that were much less—low end properties with qualities that could satisfy the need for long-term successful investing. It wasn't long before she happily went ahead and purchased a small one-bedroom flat priced at $55,000, returning $120 a week. After this hurdle had been overcome, she found it much easier to move on, still maintaining an upper limit for her investing with which she felt comfortable. She may not get rich quickly but there is a good chance she will get rich slowly!

The money you commit to any one property has to be within your own comfort zone. Don't make the mistake of believing, however, that you need to spend up big in order to achieve success. In fact, the reverse can be true. Take, as an example, an investor with $450,000 to invest. This investor can buy one property for $450,000, or three at $150,000 each.

The investor choosing to buy one property at $450,000 has put all of his eggs in one basket. He has placed all of his hopes into this one property delivering the capital gain he needs and hopefully the cash flow in the short term, although higher priced property is rarely cash flow positive. The pay-off will be an increase to the value at whatever the current rate of gain is for that particular area, but if the investor has chosen incorrectly then this hoped for gain may not materialise completely. While a 10 per cent increase would see a gain of $45,000, a 5 per cent increase would see a gain of only $22,500.

The investor buying three properties can spread the investment. She can buy in three different areas and even buy three different property types. In doing so, she is increasing her exposure to a variety of possible outcomes. Like the first investor, if all three experience growth of 10 per cent, she will see a gain of $45,000. If all three only experience a 5 per cent growth, she will see a gain of $22,500. So far everything is equal.

However, it is far more likely she will see a mix of gains and a mix of returns. Property cannot be treated as one single entity when it comes to possible gain. While average gain across a nation may be 9 per cent for the year, this may be made up of 15 per cent in one area and perhaps only 3 per cent in another. The person spreading her investing has increased her chances of accessing this range of gains. She may see 12 per cent on one, 8 per cent on another and 5 per cent on the third, giving her a nice average of around 8.5 per cent. In addition, this investor has far more flexibility—any vacancy is unlikely to affect the entire portfolio at once, and should she need to liquidate there is the option of only selling part of the portfolio and keeping the rest. As there are more buyers in this market, liquidation would be easier. As there are also more tenants in this market, she may be less likely to experience vacancy while she holds the property.

Be aware of what your own needs are in terms of comfort and safety

Be aware of what your own needs are in terms of comfort and safety and commit to what you would like to spend before you begin looking. Stick to this commitment and you will be sure to take a little of the stress out of the process and go forward with renewed confidence.

How would niche market property impact on my portfolio?

As you have been able to see from Chapter 2 and my prior books, niche market properties can provide an excellent cash flow and enhance the ability to leverage through the quicker reduction of debt. Many of these properties maintain their high cash flow for years after their purchase and they can enjoy excellent occupancy rates if they have been well chosen and well managed.

There can be problems with this type of property, however, and if you choose to include a niche market property in your portfolio, you must be aware of the impact it can have on the entire portfolio and perhaps your ability to leverage into further property.

At this stage, the main difficulty with niche market property is its acceptance by lenders. It can be very difficult to find a bank or non-bank lender that will willingly accept these properties as security and this can make it difficult if you are keen to buy one.

The particular difficulties you may encounter include the following:

☐ Some lenders will not accept niche market property as a security at all because they are not convinced it can experience continued success.

☐ Some lenders will only allow smaller loan-to-valuation ratios (that is the percentage of the value which can be borrowed against) due to the often smaller size of these properties and their history of static or even declining values.

❐ Most lenders will need to be convinced there is a secondary use for the property in the event that the original purpose fails, and so will reject most applications for funding if this secondary use cannot be identified.

This does not mean that you cannot include a niche market property in your portfolio. It simply means that you must do so fully aware of the true impact that such a purchase may have on your future investing.

Where you already have an abundance of equity across your portfolio, buying one of these properties may have little impact at all. One of my newer clients, Stan, came to me with owner-occupied property worth $800,000, unencumbered. He wanted to invest quite aggressively and was impressed with the returns of a few niche market properties he had seen. Even if he chose to purchase a $300,000 niche market property (using just his own home as security if his bank will not accept the niche market property), he would still have $500,000 more in security available for further borrowing. Since additional purchases are most likely to be more mainstream, he can, if he needs to, use any other purchases as additional security alongside his own home if he really wished to be aggressive with his purchases. Since you should only ever give the bank enough security to cover your debts, Stan has quite a lot of room on his existing home for the next three or four purchases—he need not provide any additional security at all. However, if you are in a different situation, issues you must consider are:

❐ Where your current equity is lower, you may need to use a non-mainstream lender that may provide funding for the property you have chosen; however, this could come at a premium in the form of slightly higher interest rates or a high establishment fee. Where the property has a high cash flow, this is probably not a big issue for you, but do be certain there will be no impact on your lifestyle.

❑ Where you have low equity and you choose a property on which a lender will only allow a low loan-to-valuation ratio, it could be that you either cannot proceed due to your inability to raise sufficient funds, or to do so would use up all of your equity. This may become a problem if the niche market property also grows slowly, as the burden for future leverage will rest solely with your other property(s).

❑ Where you buy a property that no bank will accept as security and you have used up all of your equity to do so (effectively providing only existing property as security), be aware that while your entire portfolio (including this new property) may gain value, it will only be the increased value of the accepted property which you can use to leverage into more property. Under these circumstances, the purchase of this niche market property may slow up the speed with which you can invest, unless the cash flow is high enough to pay down debt and so speed up equity acquisition.

There is nothing wrong with buying niche market property. Just because the banks do not like it does not make it a bad investment—bank policies are traditionally slow to change and the powers that be do not always know the best thing for you when it comes to your investing future.

When I first considered assisting one of my clients with the purchase of a retirement unit, one of the major lenders steadfastly refused to consider lending for this purpose. This particular development was essentially just a complex of one-bedroom apartments, with each one lot sized well over 50 square metres. The on-site manager chose to market this particular complex to the seniors market—no real aged facilities were provided, there was certainly no government accreditation and, in fact, anyone could live there, including the owners themselves if they chose to. No matter how many ways we presented this property to the bank, they stood fast with their policy—no lending on retirement complexes. We tried to argue that in real terms this was not even a retirement complex, but we just couldn't win. While many people making the policies in large institutions don't have their fingers on the pulse in terms of viable investing opportunities, I feel that policies like this will certainly see major changes in the coming years as favour for this type of investing grows.

As mentioned, niche market investments can be very successful. Just be sure you make purchases such as these with your eyes wide open and explore the true future impact on you before making any decisions or signing any contracts.

How do I manage my capital gains tax liability?

Since property is an investment, you are liable to pay capital gains tax on any realised gain in the same way a share or managed fund investor is. Chapter 5 covers the way that capital gains tax is calculated, based on when you purchase and dispose of your property.

When people sell property, they often overestimate the real gain on that property because they omit the capital gains tax liability. I often smile when I see the television property shows that highlight the smart young couple who bought a property for $400,000, spent six months full time and $100,000 renovating to sell again for $560,000. It always sounds like a great result but by the time you take into account the selling costs and the capital gains tax, it usually turns out to be a pretty poor hourly rate of pay for these people who for the length of the renovation have committed their entire lives and often the favours of many friends to the project.

Capital gains tax is a fact of life (for now at least) and so a cost of investing that must be accounted for in your calculations. This does not mean, however, that it is not important to understand how you can lessen the impact of capital gains tax with a little forward planning.

Let's take Joshua, Natalie and Frederick as three prime examples. All three are colleagues working for the same company at the same rate of pay, which is $65,000 a year. They are good friends who do many things together, including building their investment portfolios. They reach the stage where they all have five properties, each valued at \$200,000, having been purchased for \$100,000 each (averaged for ease of calculation). All three investors choose to pay interest-only on their investment debts.

Joshua decides that now is the best time for him to liquidate all of his property, as he would like to take a holiday and perhaps invest elsewhere. He sells the entire portfolio with the following result, as shown in the table below.

Sale price	\$1,000,000
Sale costs	\$5,000
Agent's commissions	\$35,000
Net receipts	\$960,000
Original costs	\$500,000
Profit	\$460,000
CGT at 47% on half	\$108,100
Net Profit to Joshua	**\$351,900**

Natalie decides to wait until she has retired and is not earning an income to liquidate her property. Without considering the extra growth (and so extra net profit) she would make by delaying the sales, the result for Natalie is shown overleaf.

Natalie has managed to save a little of the tax by waiting until she had no other income before liquidating her property.

Frederick decides to liquidate his property one at a time, each year after he retires. Without considering the extra growth (and so extra net profit) he would make by delaying the sales, his results would be as shown overleaf.

Sale price	$1,000,000
Sale costs	$5,000
Agent's commissions	$35,000
Net receipts	$960,000
Original costs	$500,000
Profit	$460,000
CGT on half (0 – $6,000: Nil $6001 – $20,000: 17% or $2,380 $20,001 – $50,000: 30% or $9,000 $50,001 – $60,000: 42% or $4,200 $60,001 – $230,000: 47% or $79,900)	
Total CGT	$95,480
Net Profit to Natalie	**$364,520**

Sale price	$200,000 (each year for 5 years)
Sale costs	$1,000 for each property
Agent's commissions	$7,000 for each property
Net receipts	$192,000
Original costs	$100,000
Profit	$92,000
CGT on half (0 – $6,000: Nil $6001 – $20,000: 17% or $2,380 $20,001 – $46,000: 30% or $7,800)	
Total CGT	$10,180 for 5 years or $50,900
Net Profit to Frederick	**$409,100**

Of course, the comparisons are far more complicated than this —for example, the value of the properties should increase the longer they are kept, those keeping their property may still be receiving an income, and the cost base must be adjusted for purchasing costs and depreciation. But the point is, prior to making any sale, you must seriously consider the impact of capital gains tax and decide whether there may be a more opportune moment in the future to effect the sale. Just as each investment strategy must be personal and based on individual financial circumstances, so must each exit strategy.

Summary

☐ A well-balanced property portfolio should have a mix of many types of property in different areas.

☐ It may be best to sell a lemon if it is holding you back from further investing.

☐ A niche market property may impact on future borrowing, so be sure you have enough borrowing capacity and sufficient equity for additional purchases before you use up equity in this way and proceed with any niche market property.

☐ You do not necessarily need an exit strategy in place when you begin investing as this will probably change as you become more astute and your personal financial circumstances change.

☐ Your exit strategy should be carefully considered to include your potential capital gains tax liability and so allow you to time your liquidation as cost-efficiently as possible.

Conclusion

So many investors buy property and then wrongly believe that the property will somehow take care of itself. While managed funds may be taken care of by other, expert managers, investment in property brings with it a responsibility which cannot be handed on.

When you buy property as an investment, you do not have any excuse to 'set and forget'. Just as the share investor must continually watch his stocks and tweak his investments from time to time, the property investor cannot afford to become complacent. Property should not be considered the lazy man's investment of choice—there is just as much work required to watch over and maintain your investment as there was when you bought it. Being aware of this and watching your market and your returns carefully will help you to ensure that you remain in the best possible position at all times.

5   Maximising your cash flow

❐ You may have more claimable items than you realise

❐ Many tax law changes have altered the way in which you can make some claims

❐ Knowing more than your accountant does is a good way to be sure you maximise your cash flow

I am frequently asked to provide to investors a magic formula that will instantly turn their negatively geared properties into positive cash flow properties. Once investors begin to feel the pinch of having less cash flow than before they invested, many will come seeking a quick solution to their problem.

And while in most cases you simply cannot reverse the cash flow and repair the problems that negative cash flow can bring, I am constantly amazed at just how few people (and how few accountants) fully understand the scope that can be afforded to them by knowing and understanding depreciation allowances for investors. Sometimes, what seems like a negative cash flow investment may actually be a positive cash flow one once it is fully examined for the tax advantages it can provide.

Some months ago, I was interviewed on a national radio program alongside another author of property books. It quickly became apparent that we had two very different opinions on how to invest in property, and as the debate became a little heated the announcer became more excited, as discord between guests always makes great radio.

The other guest insisted that there was no such thing as positive cash flow property, despite my reassurances that I had it in my own portfolio (must be just one of my wild fantasies!). I patiently explained how on-paper costs such as depreciation could enhance an investment and provide valuable cash flow.

"Rubbish!" he countered. "You don't think the tax office is stupid do you? The only reason they let you claim depreciation is because you eventually have to replace those items!" Well, obviously, but if you are going to have to replace the items anyway, why not claim the depreciation on them? It's not as if not claiming the depreciation somehow makes the items last longer!

Tax benefits are the icing, the cream, the plate and probably the spoon you use to eat the cake too!

While growth investors will tell you that tax benefits are simply the icing on the cake, I believe they are the icing, the cream, the plate and probably the spoon you use to eat it too!

With this in mind, in this chapter I would like to provide in-depth information about the kinds of things you can claim as a tax deduction and the ways in which your claims can be made. While it would certainly take an entire book to cover the full complement of possible tax deductions available on any investment property, hopefully this will enable you to look to your own property and determine if there is anything you have missed, or prepare you for any new property you may purchase.

Claiming in a nutshell

When you earn an income from any source, you will pay tax and the amount of tax you pay depends on the amount of income you have earned within a financial year. At the time of writing, the tax rates for Australia are as shown in the table below.

On the first $6,000	nil tax to be paid
$6,001–$21,600	17¢ in every dollar earned
$21,601–$52,000	30¢ in every dollar earned
$52,001–$62,500	42¢ in every dollar earned
$62,500 +	47¢ in every dollar earned

There will also be the Medicare levy to pay, depending on the income earned. I am always a little confused by people who say that they do not want a pay rise as it will put them in the next tax bracket. It's as if they believe that when you are pushed over into the next bracket the new tax applies to the whole salary, in effect making you earn less as a net income. This is, of course, not true. As the table above shows, each dollar incurs tax at the rate applied to the category into which it falls.

When you earn income from a property, your gross income increases. To lessen the burden of paying additional tax from this new gross income, the tax department allows you to deduct all of the costs associated with the property, providing they were directly related to the earning of income on that property. It will also let you deduct an amount which represents the depreciation on items in your property and the depreciation on the actual building itself. The best thing about being allowed to deduct this amount is that these items do not have ongoing costs related to them—that is, they are on paper and do not actually represent any money you must pay on an ongoing basis.

If you own a negatively geared property where you have income from rent, actual costs from the property but no on-paper deductions, the taxable amount you have after you consider these items will be less than it was before you had the property, and so you are required to pay less tax than you used to pay. This is provided to you either as a lump sum at the end of the year or weekly in your pay packet if you have made an income tax variation request to your employer during the year. However, negatively geared investors will also have more costs than they had before they bought the property, so although they do pay less tax, the extra money received from this is not enough to cover the shortfall, and the 'in-hand' income is reduced.

If you own positively geared property with no on-paper deductions, the income you receive from the property will be greater than the actual costs and you will have a higher taxable income, resulting in you having an additional tax liability. You can either elect to pay this at the end of the year or spread these payments over the year by submitting a request to vary tax form.

If you own property with on-paper deductions, it is likely these deductions will make it appear that your income is less than it was before you invested (that is, shows an on-paper loss), and so you will receive tax back. Since you only have to pay out actual costs on the property, not the value of the depreciation, the tax back can often be more than you need to meet the shortfall, and you get to keep whatever is left over.

What can you claim?

The things that you can claim are separated into three categories —capital costs, revenue costs and depreciation.

Capital costs

This includes all of the amounts which you must pay out to actually purchase, sell or improve your property. They include:

☐ government purchase stamp duties

☐ agent's commissions

☐ conveyancing costs, such as search fees, solicitors' charges and sundries

☐ building improvements of a capital nature (not repairs)

❏ additions

❏ renovations

❏ driveways and pergolas.

With the exception of loan establishment fees, which can be claimed over a five-year period, these items are not claimed against your tax and do not provide an immediate tax deduction. What they do is reduce your gain for tax purposes and so lessen the amount of capital gains tax you ultimately pay upon sale. Let us look at the following examples.

Cheryl buys a 20-year-old property valued at $150,000. She pays $3,740 in stamp duties and $1,875 in conveyancing costs. She sells the property four years later for $175,000 and pays $6,125 to an agent to do so, as well as $1,400 for conveyancing. From the sale, Cheryl may pay the following in capital gains tax:

Sale price	$175,000
less stamp duty	$3,740
less conveyancing	$3,275
less commissions	$6,125
less purchase price	$150,000
Actual gain	$11,860
Capital gains tax on half of the gain (assuming Cheryl pays tax at 47¢ in the dollar)	**$2,787**

You can see that Cheryl is only liable to pay tax on half of the actual gain (see section on capital gains tax later in this chapter), after her costs have been considered.

Martin bought an older property in 1990 for $100,000. His conveyancing costs were $1,575 and stamp duty was $1,990. In 2001, he spent $30,000 adding a room. He sold the property in 2003 for $170,000, paying $5,950 to an agent and $1,400 in conveyancing. The capital gains tax (expressed simply here) Martin may pay is shown below.

Sale price	$170,000
less stamp duty	$1,990
less conveyancing	$1,575
less commissions	$5,950
less cost of building	$30,000
less purchase price	$100,000
Actual gain	$30,485
Capital gains tax on half the gain (assuming Martin pays tax at 47¢ in the dollar)	**$7,164**

In reality, although this property was outside the allowable period to claim depreciation, Martin would be allowed to claim depreciation on the addition during the period he held the property, and as such his calculations for capital gains tax would have been a little more complex at the time of sale. This will be covered in more detail later in this chapter.

Revenue costs

When you own an investment property, you are allowed to claim the cost of maintaining that property as a tax deduction. In effect, for every dollar you spend on costs that are directly associated with earning an income, you will get back tax at whatever marginal rate you pay. Sometimes, the claims may be high enough to reduce your taxable income to a lower bracket—so, for example, you may have $15,000 worth of costs to claim but if you earn a gross income of $57,000, you can claim $5,000 of these costs at 42 per cent (giving you back tax of $2,100) and $10,000 of these costs at 30 per cent (giving you back tax of $3,000). From this example, you can see why negative gearing can be more beneficial to those with more of their income in the higher brackets.

The kinds of actual costs you can claim as a tax deduction include:

- ☐ loan interest costs and bank fees, including interest on loans taken out to purchase depreciating assets for the property, carry out renovations or effect repairs
- ☐ property management costs, including letting fees, management fees, inspection fees, advertising and sundries
- ☐ repair bills, as long as the repairs are not actual improvements or capital costs
- ☐ rates, both water and council
- ☐ energy costs
- ☐ telephone costs
- ☐ land tax
- ☐ body corporate fees
- ☐ the owner's costs of travel reasonably associated with two inspections a year—if you combine a holiday with this inspection, this will impact on the claim you can make
- ☐ pest control
- ☐ security patrol
- ☐ quantity surveyor's costs
- ☐ garden and property maintenance, and cleaning
- ☐ the costs incurred when borrowing over a five-year period (or the period that the investment is held), including establishment fees, stamp duty on the loan, solicitor's costs, lender's mortgage insurance and valuation costs
- ☐ landlord's and building and contents insurance, public liability insurance.

All of these costs must be paid out before they can be claimed, and you can only ever get back as much as your marginal rate of tax on each dollar spent.

It is important to be in tune with what the tax department calls 'purpose', and with 'responsibility' for costs. If you are unsure of whether a cost can be claimed or not, ask yourself the following two questions:

1   Was this cost related in its entirety to earning an income?

2   Who paid the cost?

If the answer to the first question is yes and you paid these costs, you can probably claim them. However, if it is yes and someone else, such as the tenant, has paid the costs, you cannot claim them.

It could be that you only paid part of a cost, or only part of it related to earning an income. Under these circumstances, that portion of the cost which you paid or which related to the part of your property that produced an income is the portion you are able to claim.

Depreciation

When you own any real estate, usually its value increases, or appreciates, over time. You may be interested to know that it is really the land component of your investment which is appreciating, while the building, fixtures and fittings actually lose value over time.

As the tax office is aware that these items do depreciate while you hold them, they willingly make allowances for this by providing the opportunity for you to 'write-off' these depreciating items over a period of years, to a point where they no longer have value. In a sense, this writing-off then gives you the opportunity to prepare financially for the time when they may have to be replaced. Where construction of the building is concerned, an investor selling the property prior to replacing the building (as would most commonly occur)

The land component of your investment is really what is appreciating, while the building, fixtures and fittings actually lose value over time must make an allowance upon sale for the fact that he or she received payment for an item which, on paper, was worth less than when it was purchased. It is for this reason that, upon sale, an add-back of the written-down value must be made to the gain if the building has not been replaced. This adding back of 'special building write-off' was covered in detail in *How to Create an Income for Life*. There are those people who believe that, since you must effectively 'pay back' this depreciation you should not claim it in the first place. However, *How to Create an Income for Life* gave excellent examples which show you will still be in a better position if you claim the depreciation when you are allowed to, even if some has to be repaid upon sale.

From July 2001, the uniform capital allowance (UCA) system applies to most depreciating assets, including those acquired before that date. The UCA consolidates a range of former capital allowance provisions by providing a set of general rules that apply across a variety of depreciating assets and certain other capital expenditure. Depreciation is divided into two main categories: special building write-off and plant and equipment.

Special building write-off (division 43 allowance)

Special building write-off is the allowable amount you may claim every year in deference to the decreasing value of the building. The allowable amount varies according to the type of building and when it was constructed, as follows:

❏ Short-term accommodation for travellers built between 22 August 1979 and 19 July 1982: 2.5 per cent of the construction costs for 40 years.

❏ Short term or commercial buildings built between 20 July 1982 and 17 July 1985: 2.5 per cent for those buildings constructed prior to 21 August 1984 and 4 per cent (for 25 years) for buildings constructed between 22 August 1984 and 15 September 1987.

❏ Residential buildings constructed before 18 July 1985: there is no allowable claim for buildings where construction began before this date.

❏ Residential construction occurring between 18 July 1985 and 15 September 1987: 4 per cent of the cost of construction, over a period of 25 years. Note that the 25 years start from the date of construction so, if you purchased a property such as this in 2003, for example, you may only have about 7 years of depreciation left to claim.

❏ Residential construction occurring after 15 September 1987: 2.5 per cent of the original construction costs over a 40-year period. In 2003, the shortest time left for property built after this date would be 24 years.

❏ Tourist accommodation built between 18 July 1985 and 15 September 1987: short-term let property available for minimum stays of one night, with available restaurant facilities and single key access qualifies for 4 per cent depreciation over a 25-year period.

❏ Tourist accommodation built between 15 September 1987 and 26 February 1992: 2.5 per cent for 40 years. The allowance increases back to 4 per cent for 25 years for properties built after this time.

❏ Structural improvements carried out after 26 February 1992: 2.5 per cent for 40 years. So, where a property built before the allowable dates has had structural renovations after February 1992, the cost of these renovations may be depreciated.

Opposite is a quick ready reference table to assist you to easily identify the deductibility of your property.

You do not have to buy the property new in order to qualify for the special building write-off claim. If you buy an established property, you are eligible to claim the balance of the unclaimed special building write-off. Where the prior owner has not claimed anything, you are still only allowed to claim what would have been the balance—so a property built for an owner occupier in 1993 and bought by an investor in 2003 has 30 years remaining for allowable claims of special building write-off.

Property and Dates	None	2.5%	4%
Short term or commercial			
before 22 August 1979	☑		
22 Aug 1979–19 Aug 1982		☑	
20 July 1982–21 Aug 1984			☑
22 Aug 1984–15 Sept 1987			☑
Residential buildings ⓧ			
before 18 July 1985	☑		
18 July 1985–15 Sept 1987			☑
15 Sept 1987–current		☑	
Tourist accommodation			
18 July 1985–15 Sept 1987			☑
15 Sept 1987–26 Feb 1992		☑	
26 Feb 1992–current			☑
Structural improvements			
after 26 Feb 1992		☑	

Special building write-off applies to the building itself and its associated assets which are considered part of the setting for the rent producing activity rather than assets in their own right. It includes:

❑ architect's fees, engineering fees and excavation costs

❑ payments to carpenters, builders, bricklayers and other tradespeople

❑ construction of retaining walls, fences and pools

❑ built-in kitchen cupboards

❑ clothes hoists

❑ doors and window fittings

❑ driveways and paths

❑ electrical wiring

❑ fencing and retaining walls

❑ floor and wall tiles

❑ garages and non-portable sheds

❏ in-ground swimming pools, spas and saunas

❏ plumbing and gas fittings

❏ reticulation piping

❏ roller doors and shutters

❏ roof-top ventilators and skylights

❏ security doors and screens that are permanently fixed to the building

❏ sinks, tubs and baths

❏ wash basins and toilet bowls.

Items not included are:

❏ cost of the land

❏ expenditure on clearing the land

❏ permanent earthworks that are not integral to the building

❏ landscaping

❏ builder's profit margin, if established.

Plant and equipment depreciation

The property you buy is likely to include a number of items that are not considered a part of the special building write-off. Generally speaking, if the item cannot be moved, it is part of the construction, and so forms part of the total value of the building. Where an item may be removed easily, it is considered to be plant or equipment—or a fixture, fitting or piece of furniture. The list of possible items is endless, but generally includes:

❏ all items of furniture contained inside the house and used as part of the letting activity, such as tables, chairs, beds, lamps, kitchen appliances and kitchenware

❏ blinds and venetians

❏ curtains, carpets and drapes

❏ garbage units

❏ hot water services

- ❏ lawn mowers
- ❏ linoleums and other floor coverings
- ❏ microwave ovens
- ❏ radios
- ❏ refrigerators
- ❏ stoves
- ❏ televisions sets, videos, DVDs, CDs
- ❏ vacuum cleaners
- ❏ washing machines and dryers.

Anything which can be removed and replaced will be considered to be a part of the plant and equipment, and so be eligible for some kind of claim.

There are two ways you can claim depreciation on these items. They are the diminishing value method and the prime cost method.

The diminishing value method is where the deduction is calculated by assuming that the decline in value each year is a proportion of the remaining value and produces a progressively smaller decline over time. The formula for calculating depreciation using this method is:

$$\text{Base Value} \quad \times \quad \frac{\text{Days owned}}{365} \quad \times \quad \frac{150\%}{\text{Effective life}}$$

The 'effective life' of a depreciable item is the term used to describe the period over which it is accepted that an item will actually last. Effective life is expressed in years, including fractions of years—it is not rounded to the nearest whole year. The commissioner of taxation publishes a table of accepted life spans for the more common items against which you can make a claim. However, if investors have evidence to suggest that a different life span should be given to any one item, they are free to make the claim for the life they believe the item should have, as long as this claim can be substantiated.

For example, I have a house by the beach which is holiday-let. While carpets would normally be given an effective life of ten years, I believe it is reasonable for me to apply a life of just five years for the carpets in this house. This is because not only is there harsher than usual wear and tear from holiday tenants, but its location near the beach means that sand is constantly being traipsed in and out, shortening the life of the carpet.

To illustrate the diminishing value method, take as an example a removable spa, the original cost of which to the owner was $4,000 and which the tax department accepts a life span of five years for. Year one claims would be as follows:

$4,000   x   1 (owned for the entire year)   x   30%   = $1,200

In year two, the claim would be:

$2,800   x   1 (owned for the entire year)   x   30%   = $840

The claim in year three would be $588, $412 in year four, and so on. Once the written-down value of the spa fell below $1,000, it is likely that it would be allocated to a low-value pool (see section on low-value pooling).

The prime cost method of depreciation assumes that the value of a depreciating asset decreases uniformly over its effective life, as per the following formula:

$$\text{Cost} \quad \times \quad \frac{\text{Days owned}}{365} \quad \times \quad \frac{100\%}{\text{Effective life}}$$

Using the spa above as an example, year one claim would be:

$4,000   ×   1   ×   20%   = $800

Each subsequent year would have the same claim allowed.

It is up to the investor to decide which method he or she prefers to use; however, once chosen the same method must be applied each year. Clearly, investors with a cash flow which is heavily impacted by loss of tax benefits would do best to choose the prime cost method as this allows them to maintain a more static amount of deductions over the effective life of the items being claimed.

Low-value pooling

From July 2001, an optional low-value pooling arrangement for plant was introduced. It applies to certain plant having a cost of less than $1,000 or an undeducted value of less than $1,000. This plant can now be allocated to a low-value pool and depreciated at statutory rates.

The assets which you may allocate to this pool include low-cost assets, which are items that have a cost at the end of the first year of less than $1,000, and low-value assets that have an adjusted opening value of less than $1,000.

Once you choose to create a low-value pool, you must allocate all low-cost assets to this pool in that year and in every subsequent year. However, this rule does not apply to low-value assets and you can choose whether you will allocate a particular low-value asset to the pool or not.

Once you have created this pool, it is not necessary to calculate the decline in value of each individual asset held within it—you simply calculate one amount for the decline in value of all of the assets in the pool. The deduction for this decline in value is worked out using a diminishing value of 37.5 per cent.

Items under $300

When you buy a property, be it new or already established, it will most probably contain a number of items the cost or value of which at purchase is less than $300. Any such item may be written–off in the first year—that is, the entire value is claimed at once and it is considered to have an effective life of just that one year. Be very careful of this one though—you are not able to break down item groups into single items. For example, if the total value of lighting was, say, $1,000 and this comprised 20 $50 lights, you would only be permitted to claim the $1,000 over the effective life of lighting by either the prime cost method or the diminishing value method. You are not able to write off each $50 light in its first year. If the item is part of a set of items which you have either bought or started to buy, the total value of the set must not exceed $300 to be eligible for 100 per cent first year write off.

What if no-one knows the original costs?

It is highly likely that you will buy property which contains many items for which the previous owner has not made any claims. In this case, it would be most unlikely for the investor to know what the costs of his or her construction, furniture, fixtures and fittings were unless the previous owner kept detailed records of this from when the property was built.

Where it is impossible for an investor to determine the true value of claimable items any other way, it is acceptable to the tax department for the investor to retain the services of a quantity surveyor. For a cost of around $500, a quantity surveyor will prepare a 'depreciation schedule' for you. This schedule will not only provide a cost estimate of the original building (allowing you to then claim the balance of the special building write-off for the remaining years), it will determine a new effective life for all of the plant and equipment contained within. In essence, you are given the value as at time of your purchase of the plant and equipment, and you will be allowed to begin a new effective life for these items. Where an item is second-hand, however, the effective life may differ from the effective lives published by the commissioner of taxation, and you may need to make reasonable estimates of your own. If you do this, be sure to keep accurate records of the estimates you make and the basis on which you made them.

Pro rata claiming

You are not allowed to claim expenses on any property not actively used for income production (such as vacant land and holiday homes not let out). If you own property that is used for income production for part of the year, there may be occasions where you need to apportion your expenses between deductible and non-deductible claims. The following examples may help you determine deductibility of your own property and its assets.

Sacha and Jacob have a holiday house they like to use throughout the year. During the school holidays, however, they make this available for others to lease. They must calculate the period of time the house is unavailable for lease as a percentage of the year. In this case, they make this house available for ten weeks a year, or 19.2% of the year. Therefore, only 19.2% of all expenses, depreciation and special building write-off are able to be claimed, while 100% of all income must be declared.

Bob owns a property that is partly let. He occupies the main house, which comprises eight rooms, and lets out four rooms permanently to tenants. He is allowed to claim 33% of his general expenses, as well as a reasonable amount for his tenants' access to common areas such as garages and outdoor areas.

Charlotte has a unit in Townsville and each year she takes a holiday to inspect this property. She spends one day inspecting the property and six days enjoying the holiday. Under these circumstances the purpose for her trip is actually the holiday. It is unlikely she would succeed with a claim for the airfares, although she may claim the costs of the one day—including taxi fares and possibly one night's accommodation.

If the property is not available for a tenant 365 days a year, the claimant must apportion the expenses. If, on the other hand, the property is available but suffers periods of vacancy, the full expenses can still be claimed.

Division of claims between joint owners

The way that claims are divided between joint owners depends on the nature of the ownership (see Chapter 6—Comprehensive

Structures). The following examples show the different ways that claims can be made.

Florence and Floyd own four properties as joint tenants. They must declare 50% of the income each and they can claim 50% of all expenses and on-paper deductions each.

Tammy and Clarence own three properties as tenants in common. The title deeds show that Tammy owns 75% of each and Clarence 25%. Tammy must declare 75% of all income and may claim 75% of all expenses and on-paper deductions while Clarence is responsible for 25% of them.

The Joneses own ten properties as joint tenants, and Mrs Jones earns income from employment which is much higher than Mr Jones. As she is the higher income earner, they draw up a partnership agreement stating that Mrs Jones is essentially liable to pay more of the expenses, and therefore they have an 80/20 partnership. At tax time, Mrs Jones wants to claim 80% of the rental loss. However, they are not allowed to do so as the partnership agreement cannot change their interest in the property, which is 50/50 at law due to the joint tenancy.

The Frosts own six properties as joint tenants. They carry out a fair bit of the work involved in letting these properties and much of the cleaning and maintenance. The main source of their income remains their full-time jobs, however. Although they are heavily involved in these properties, they are not considered to be carrying out a 'rental property' business and so have no opportunity to change the portions which each may claim, which remains at 50% each.

Zelda and Craig own three blocks of eight units and 14 duplexes. While they have other investment income, their entire livelihood is derived from the upkeep of these properties. Some of their properties are owned as joint tenants and some as tenants in common with a variety of splits. They have a partnership agreement which makes them partners at law and they have elected to apportion 75% of income, expenses and deductions to Craig, whose personal exertion in this activity is greater than Zelda's.

They are allowed to make their claims using this same apportionment for four reasons:

1. the size and scale of their rental property activities
2. the number of hours they spend on this activity
3. their personal involvement in the activities
4. the businesslike manner in which the activities are planned, organised and carried out.

All four reasons indicate that a person is actually carrying on the business of investing in properties, rather than investing in property for investment sake alone.

You can see from the examples that the way you can claim is quite clear cut, and you should make sure the way you plan to make your claims is allowable within tax laws.

When you no longer hold an asset

If you cease to hold or use a depreciating asset, it is considered that a 'balancing adjustment' event has occurred. This happens when:

❐ you stop holding the asset because it is sold, lost or destroyed

❐ you stop using the asset

❐ a change occurs in the ownership of the asset.

When one of these events occurs you are required to determine the termination value of that asset and its adjustable (or written-down) value as at the time of the event. If the termination value is greater than the adjustable value, you must include the difference in your assessable income. If it is less, you may claim this as a loss against your income.

Prepaying interest and expenses

You might choose to 'prepay' some of the interest on your investment loan or some of the expenses that you may incur in the following year. An investor would choose to do this where he or she has made a profit from positive gearing in one year but expects that the situation may change for the following year.

Investors are allowed to prepay up to 12 months of interest expenses providing the period ends on or before 30 June in the following year. They may then claim this as an immediate deduction. Before choosing to do this, be sure that the amount you are choosing to pay falls within the allowable limits, and that there really is a long-term benefit.

Capital gains tax

As mentioned in a Chapter 4, any gain realised upon the sale of a property which was purchased after 19 September 1985 will incur a capital gains tax liability. The rate at which you must pay capital gains tax depends on when you acquired the property.

If you purchased the property after 19 September 1985 but prior to 21 September 1999, you must pay capital gains tax on the gain you realise after the purchase price has been indexed. The formula for calculating your liability is as follows.

Sale price minus costs to sell

minus

Indexed purchase price minus claimed
special building write-off, plus costs to buy

equals

Gain multiplied by marginal rate of tax

equals

Capital gains tax liability

Note that this method of calculating your liability allows for the fact that the actual value of the dollars you used to buy the property in the first place has decreased over time, and so the original purchase price is indexed to take this into account. In addition, your purchase and sale costs are also considered, meaning that you effectively only pay tax on the true gain, at your highest marginal rate of tax.

If your purchase was made after 21 September 1999 and you hold the asset for more than 12 months, you will not be allowed to index the purchase price but you will only have to pay tax on half of the gain, after purchase and sale costs are considered. To calculate your liability, use the formula on the previous page but do not index the purchase price and apply your marginal rate of tax to just half of the net gain.

If your purchase has been held for a period of less than 12 months, you are not able to apply any method of discounting to your capital gains. You must pay capital gains tax on the full amount.

If you purchased prior to 21 September 1999, you have the choice as to which method you use so calculate which one is the most beneficial for you on each property that you choose to liquidate, and use it.

It is useful to note that capital gains tax can apply to property you acquired from a deceased estate and subsequently disposed of, although in some cases the 12 month rule may not apply. If you have such property, consult with an accountant prior to disposal so that you are prepared for any tax which may arise.

Capital losses

If you incur a capital loss from an asset you dispose of, you may offset this loss against any other capital gain you may make

If you incur a capital loss from an asset you dispose of, you may offset this loss against any other capital gain you may make. If you are eligible for a discount on your capital gains tax via one of the methods outlined above, you must apply the loss to the gain before applying the discount.

If you did not make any capital gains in the year in which you made a loss, or if you made a greater loss than a gain, you may carry forward your losses to offset against capital gains in future years. To do this, you must keep accurate records.

Keeping records

The tax office requires that you keep records relating to your rental property for a period of five years from when you lodge your tax return. If you purchase or inherit a property or otherwise receive property as part of a settlement, you must begin to keep records immediately.

These records must set out:

❏ the exact date the asset was acquired

❏ the exact date of disposal and the amount received for the sale

❏ any amount which may form part of a cost base

❏ records relating to income received

❏ records relating to costs incurred

❏ any surveyors reports that have been prepared.

Estimates and guesses are rarely accepted without some form of substantiation.

Summary

❏ Some costs are claimable each year while others can only be offset against capital gains upon sale.

❏ Special building write-off differs according to the type of property and the year it was constructed.

❏ Low-value pooling allows items of low value to be claimed at statutory rates.

❏ Items under $300 can be claimed 100 per cent in year one.

❐ Where a property is not used 100 per cent of the time to produce an income, only pro rata claims can be made for expenses and on-paper deductions.

❐ Claims must be apportioned according to the legal interest in the property.

❐ Interest on a property can be prepaid for 12 months and claimed in the year in which it is paid.

❐ Capital gains tax will apply upon disposal of the asset.

Conclusion

So there you have it—the icing on the cake (and the cream), so to speak! Always remember that sometimes the icing is the best part. This little bit extra may well be the very thing which allows you to continue to invest without experiencing financial difficulty or lifestyle changes today. Learn as much as you can about tax and allowable claims so that you can be sure your accountant is making the correct claims for you. And lastly, be aware that in a self-assessing taxation system the onus is on you to ensure your claims are correct. Even if someone else—including your accountant—helps you complete your tax return, you are still legally responsible for the accuracy of the information.

6 Comprehensive property structures

❐ Properties can be bought as individuals, in a trust or in corporate structures

❐ Once a property purchase structure is chosen and finalised it is very hard to change in most states

❐ Income today and in the future must be considered before deciding in whose name to purchase

❐ In some cases, the tax office will see through a structure if it does not fall within tax office rules

When you buy property as an investment, most often you will be making this purchase from a real estate agent, a developer or his or her agent, or a property marketer. While many of these people may be very good at their job, it is important for you to be aware of what their job is—to sell property. They will be familiar with the sales and conveyancing process and many of the selling points of the property, but it will be highly unlikely that their expertise will extend to the ability to provide sound advice in regards to the structure within which it is most effective for you to purchase.

In previous books I have covered the benefits and drawbacks for people with partners of investing in just one name or in joint names, and how to decide which one is right for you both at the time of investing and beyond. Since then, I have been inundated with questions from graduates of get-rich-quick seminars asking me why I never talk to investors about buying property in a company name or within a discretionary trust structure.

Probably the main reason is more related to the fact that I like to try to keep investing simple for people than to anything else. While I would never suggest that many investors would not be able to understand complex approaches, I do know that with our lives as busy as they are today, the last thing we really need is to become involved in a complicated structure which we may not fully understand, and one where the actual costs may well outweigh the benefits. Add to that the fact that the laws are ever-changing in these areas, meaning a structure you choose for today may well become less beneficial or outdated in the future.

I have had many clients come to me with extremely complex and fragmented structures, with property bought in a range of names, trusts and company structures. These investors have usually taken the advice of the person selling the property, or followed information received at the latest get-rich-quick seminar. If you are to be successful with your own investing both now and in times to come, it is important that you are aware of the kinds of structures which are being suggested to investors today and how you can become involved, so that you can better understand if one of these may be appropriate for you.

These structures include:

- corporate structures
- family trusts
- superannuation funds
- WRAPs
- joint names vs single names
- joint tenants vs tenants in common.

This chapter will examine the benefits and drawbacks of these structures.

Corporate structures

Often it is suggested that an investor set up a company structure, or a corporation, and buy any property investments within this company. The major reason why this structure is suggested is that company tax, as at the time of writing, is 30 per cent at its highest rate. Therefore, if income is being earned from a property by a company, the most tax which would ever be paid would be 30 per cent.

Once company income is drawn by any director or individual, it becomes taxable at that person's highest marginal rate of tax

While this may seem most effective, the reality is that at the commencement of the arrangement the reverse will also be true—where the property is fully geared, the company having borrowed to effect the purchase, the maximum tax benefit to the individual would be 30 per cent. And, while most investors earn the bulk of their income from employment in the 30 per cent tax bracket, it doesn't take many property purchases to push you into higher brackets. Once in a higher bracket (or if you are already in this bracket before investing), owning property as an individual may well be more beneficial (due to the higher claims which can be made) than owning property as a company.

Once the property is paid off and becomes positively geared, the opportunity to pay tax at just 30 per cent is a tempting one. Again there are problems here, mostly experienced when it comes to actually using that income. Income only attracts tax at the company rate while it is earned and held by the company. Once it is drawn by any director or individual, it becomes taxable at that person's highest marginal rate of tax. If tax at 30 per cent has already been paid, and the individual drawing the income has tax at 47 per cent, the balance of 17 per cent must be paid.

The final issue I see as being a potential problem is that if you are setting up a company purely for the purpose of buying property, you are doing so to pay less tax. If the tax department believes that you have no other legitimate reason for having set up a company structure other than tax avoidance, it may well be within its rights to see through your company structure and treat you as an individual for tax purposes anyway. If it really was as simple as all of us going out and buying off-the-shelf companies in order to lessen our ultimate tax bill, we would all be doing it with the blessing of the tax department. In reality, it just may not be that simple, or necessarily beneficial.

Family trusts

Many years ago, self-employed people would set up a family trust to enable them to redistribute the income they earned from employment to other family members, effectively lessening the collective tax bill. The following is a typical example of how this was effected.

Len, who is a plumber, earns $60,000 net income from his business. He set up a trust to allow him to distribute $600 (tax free) to each of his five minor children ($3,000 in total) and then split the remaining $57,000 with his wife (who is not earning an income) at $28,500 each. Instead of a tax bill of $15,580 which he would have incurred had the entire earnings been paid to him, the total tax payable using his trust structure was $9,860, saving him $5,720 in tax.

A few years back the tax department moved to close up this loophole by stating that income could only be split in the above manner where there was a clear division of labour and personal exertion had been made to earn the income. It carried out random audits of trust beneficiaries and asked them what they did to earn the income they received, meaning the onus fell to these beneficiaries to prove that they actually exerted personal effort to earn this income. This effectively put paid to income splitting between spouses where one spouse played no active part in the business, and to paying children not actively involved in the business.

In addition to the ability to income split, the trust structure provided a useful shelter for assets. Trustees purchased assets in the trust and named beneficiaries who would then enjoy these assets. However, as the assets themselves were owned by the trust and not the beneficiaries, they were protected in the event that the individual (the beneficiary) was sued. The trust structure also survived death, effectively dealing with the distribution of assets by making them unavailable for distribution.

In recent times, there have been cases where, if the Australian Securities and Investments Commission believes that a trust structure was formulated purely for the purposes of sheltering assets or in contemplation of being sued, or a family court believes that assets in a trust should be split up between divorcing parties, ASIC has the power to unwind such a structure and the courts can see through the veil of the trust. There may be many reasons why a trust structure would be unwound—it could be that the individuals involved were taking part in risky ventures or knew that a business activity in which they were involved was not above board, or perhaps one spouse was trying to keep the bulk of the assets acquired during the marriage. The unwinding of these structures again meant that the individual was treated as such for both tax and any other purpose.

Since trusts do not pay tax (with income attracting tax only after it is distributed and that tax payable by the beneficiary who receives the income at their marginal rate of tax), it is unlikely that the greatest benefits of a fully geared property being held by a trust will be realised until much later in the piece, long after debt has been minimised and the property becomes positively geared (that is, income exceeds expenses and no further on-paper deductions apply). Probably the greatest benefit of a trust comes nearer the end of the investment period—as capital gains upon liquidation of property can be held within the trust and distributed to beneficiaries at a time when they can personally lessen their capital gains tax liability (perhaps in a year when they earn less income or have retired). As with any structure which you may choose, be very sure that it is right for you in the long term and not just at the beginning or end of any investment.

Superannuation funds

Since the laws governing superannuation funds have changed many times over the past ten years, we have seen an increase in the number of self-managed superannuation funds being put in place by self-employed individuals. A self-managed, or DIY, superannuation fund is one where an individual, either alone or with other parties, sets up a trust structure for the purposes of managing his or her own superannuation contributions. Often, any existing superannuation contributions held with any other fund will be rolled over into this new self-managed fund, and it is then the trustees' responsibility (who are most often also the contributors) to manage the fund and prudently invest the money.

Sometimes, due to rollover funds, superannuation funds can start with hundreds of thousands of dollars, and I have often been asked if investing in positive cash flow property is prudent for these funds.

The important point to note here is that a superannuation fund does not have the ability to borrow. Therefore, a geared strategy will not be possible and a fund can only purchase property if it is done so with cash. If the intention is to use cash to purchase property, doing so through a superannuation fund will certainly be the more effective strategy since superannuation funds enjoy concessional tax rates. However, simply contributing enough cash to a super fund with the intention of using this cash to buy property is fraught with problems, not the least of which is the fact that there is an upper limit on the amount which any one individual can contribute to superannuation in one year without being surcharged. In addition, investors should carefully consider the wisdom of using all of the cash available in the fund on one relatively illiquid investment. An alternative strategy may be to use the cash in the superannuation fund to purchase managed funds or other liquid investments, while using personal borrowing power and equity in existing property to purchase more property. Where an investor chooses to mix investments in this way and so obtain a diversified portfolio, it is an absolute must that the advice of a duly qualified and licensed financial adviser be obtained before undertaking any strategy.

WRAPs

The strategies for investing in property just seem to get more and more complex. It is no wonder that many property investors have their heads spinning and are simply not sure where to turn.

In its most basic form, a WRAP is a fairly new concept which seems to have become very popular in the US. I personally understand it best by comparing it to the 'flexi-rent' system for purchasing office equipment—you get ownership of the equipment and while you pay the rent on the equipment, your payment includes a contribution toward this ownership. At the end, you pay a pre-agreed amount based on what is considered fair market value for that item (less the contributions you have already made), which has understandably depreciated during the rental period.

A WRAP is a method of buying property where you, the individual, make the purchase using loan funds and seek a tenant (or buyer in this case) who will pay you a rent which is higher than the commitments you have on the mortgage. In this way you are essentially reselling the house to this tenant on terms finance, sort of like a package deal. Prior to the agreement being struck, you agree on a sale price which is fair market value less the contributions the tenant has already made (usually with something built in for you, who have taken the risk). In effect you, the vendor, are financing the tenants into your property until such times as they can get the finance to buy it themselves, and you have a guaranteed sale at the 'strike' price, sometimes years before it is effected. As with all deals struck prior to the event, the gamble for you is that you will underestimate the capital gain and the tenant/purchaser will be the winner. But it can go the other way, and the plan is certainly to be sure that the strike price is high enough to allow for a good gain to be made by the WRAP-er.

While WRAPs are enjoying huge success in the US, mainly due to the large deposits often needed to borrow from a bank, I personally believe that Australia may not have the market required to make such a scheme a huge success. When a person has the desire to buy property these days, there are many, many incentives, grants and offers from builders to make this dream a reality— there would seem little need for most people to enter into an agreement such as this. Where a person is unable to get finance to purchase now, this may well be due to an inability to save for a deposit at all or to a very poor credit rating, since with so many options and so much competition most people can find money somewhere. Those people who can't put together a deposit or are unable to borrow from a bank or other lender may well be the sort of tenant you really do not want, or they may be someone who cannot honour the contract to proceed with the purchase when the time comes.

If you are considering WRAPs as an option, please do your homework. Be sure only to consider tenants with clean financial histories who can demonstrate the ability to save and pay rent, and that you really can benefit from an arrangement such as this.

Joint names vs single names

How to Create an Income for Life explored the benefits and drawbacks for people with partners of choosing to buy property in either just the highest income earner's name, or in both names.

Basically, where a property is to be geared, from a tax point of view it will usually be better to buy the property in the higher income earner's name, as this person will have more tax to write-off. You must be sure, however, that this situation is likely to remain so for some time. If you can see a time in the not too distant future where the property is likely to become positively geared, the benefit for the higher income earner will only be evident in the early years. Once income exceeds expenses and this is unable to be offset by any on-paper deductions, you will want the property to be held in the name of the lower income earner, who will then pay less tax on the weekly gain.

Hence, when deciding which name you should purchase in, consider working out just how quickly you feel you can begin to eliminate debt. Try to ascertain how long you think the on-paper deductions will last by using the rule of thumb ready reckoner contained in the previous chapter.

For example, if the time in which you would like to invest is, say, 15 years, the on-paper deductions will be almost exhausted after 5 years, and you have been able to ascertain that you will eliminate enough debt to make the property positively geared, then you will wish to purchase in the name of the lower income earner. If, however, you have a large amount of possible on-paper deductions, including special building write-off which may last for another 30 to 35 years, then it may be more prudent to purchase in the name of the higher income earner. If you have estimated that there could be a change in the future to your income-earning capacity, with perhaps one partner planning to cease work or lessen their hours, then these too are important considerations. Be sure that the structure you ultimately choose is the one that will bring benefit to you for the longest period of time, which may not necessarily be the one which brings immediate benefits.

> *When deciding whether to purchase in single or joint names, be sure that the structure you choose is the one that will bring benefit to you for the longest period of time*

Joint tenants vs tenants in common

The decision to purchase as either joint tenants or tenants in common has two main bearings—one impacting on your life and one impacting after your death.

When you buy property as a joint tenant with someone else and one party dies, the remaining tenants equally share the portion owned by the deceased. As a joint tenant, you are unable to include your portion of any property purchased this way in your will, as remaining joint tenants are automatically granted ownership.

Joint tenants must also split equally any income, costs, taxation benefits or liabilities—so where there are two tenants, the split will be 50/50, where there are four it will be 25 per cent each and so on.

Tenants in common own a willable share of property. Upon death, their share of the property is said to fall within their estate and so is dealt with according to the wishes of the will. Where no will is left, these assets will fall intestate with all other assets and the decision of who they fall to rests with the courts. Tenants in common must decide at the time of purchase (noted on the title deed) the size of their share of the property. The percentage share granted to each tenant then remains forever more and determines the portion of income, expenses, tax benefits and liabilities each party is responsible for.

Beware of vendors or their agents advising you to choose a 'tenants in common' structure with say, a 99/1 per cent split, enabling the higher income earner to enjoy 99 per cent of the tax benefits while the lower income earner has a tax paid holiday every year to carry out the property inspection. Unless you have some legitimate reason for choosing such an uneven split other than to avoid tax and get the holiday, such as a predetermined legal partnership with a similar split arrangement, the tax department is well within its rights to disallow any claims for such trips or other such claims on the part of the 1 per cent owner.

Summary

❏ Corporate structures will minimise tax, but where a property is negatively geared they may not have any financial benefit for many years to come.

❏ Trust structures can be effective for protecting assets, but do not provide a great financial benefit for fully geared property purchases.

❏ As superannuation funds cannot borrow, tax effective investing only occurs where the superannuation fund uses cash to make property purchases.

❒ Wrapping is quite new in Australia and the market for such an arrangement is largely untested.

❒ If buying in one name only, be sure that this is the best choice of structure both for today and in the future.

❒ Tenants-in-common purchases allow parties to dispose of shared assets upon death according to predetermined wishes.

❒ Joint tenants always share assets equally and upon death the share of the deceased falls to the remaining tenants in equal shares.

Conclusion

No doubt in the coming years we will see many more schemes and ideas all designed to attract you as an investor to the latest expensive course or provide you with a thrilling investment ride. Many of these schemes involve the use of loopholes which are quickly closed as soon as the tax department becomes aware of them, resulting in the investor using a strategy which fast becomes unviable.

You must look holistically at your own financial circumstances and consider the impact of the ultimate structure you choose on your portfolio both today and for the rest of your life. Be aware of the potential for any investment, do your calculations and choose the structure which will have the greatest possible benefits over the longest possible time, rather than just the one which looks right today.

7 Managing each individual property

- ❐ Should you use a professional property manager?
- ❐ Understanding management rights is vital for all investors
- ❐ You will have responsibilities as a landlord which cannot be passed to someone else
- ❐ Your tenants will also have rights you must be aware of

I still haven't seen one of the properties I bought more than four years ago. When people discover that many of my properties have been bought unseen, they are usually horrified that I would consider doing such a thing. "How can you buy without looking?" they ask. I still get many emails from people who tell me that they simply could not bear to buy property without looking. I think this is an indication that not enough questions are being asked by the purchaser, and that they feel they can trust their eyes more than they can trust the words they may be hearing! As you have seen, as long as you carry out effective research, the physical appeal is going to make little difference to a property's potential to earn an income for its owner.

Imagine the added horror of others when I also tell them that most of my properties are so far away I have no hope of ever seeing them, let alone taking part in their supervision and management.

Some time ago I made a presentation in a capital city, to a group of around 250 people. Everyone seemed to enjoy the session, but of course there will always be one person who seems to want to throw down the gauntlet and undo you in front of others. When I got around to calling for questions, one gentleman stood angrily in his chair and yelled, "Of course, missy, you are not telling everyone about how tenants can destroy your asset and how property managers on the whole are a useless bunch!"

Property settlement simply marks the beginning of phase two—the very important process of getting the property competently managed and securely tenanted

Well, rather than enter into any sort of heated debate, I thanked him and told him how glad I was that he had brought these very important points to light. I then went on to explain the vital role of landlord's insurance for every property investor (outlined in detail in *How to Create an Income for Life*) and started to go through the checklist that every investor needs when choosing a property manager.

For many investors, the hope is that once settlement has occurred, a tenant will magically appear out of thin air and the property will commence providing an income. Sadly, this is rarely the case, with property settlement simply marking the beginning of phase two—the very important process of getting the property competently managed and securely tenanted. Unfortunately, all too often property management departments are run by unskilled juniors with too many properties to manage, and so problems can occur. Further, when you have purchased property far from where you live, it may not be as easy as doing the rounds and interviewing property managers.

As a property owner, it is your responsibility not only to ensure your property is effectively managed but to understand your rights as a landlord, and the rights of your tenant. This way you can have some impact on the profitability of your investment, even when it is in another town or state.

Property management

When you buy property as an investment, it will be either managed personally, managed by a professional property manager or managed on-site by an operator with either management rights, a management agreement or a leaseback deal. The features of each type of property management, along with the benefits and drawbacks, are as follows.

Managed personally

Some landlords choose to undertake property management personally. Frankly, I couldn't imagine anything worse—one of the reasons I buy property as far away from me as possible is that I don't want to be continually 'keeping an eye' on my own property and possibly having to sit helplessly by while I watch a tenant look after my property not as well as I would myself.

However, I have met investors who simply will not invest in property at all unless they can also personally manage the tenancy. If you are thinking about doing this yourself, there are many factors to consider. Not only will you need to advertise for and screen tenants, you must be responsible for the ongoing supervision and inspection of the property, rent collection, and all other duties associated with property management.

As with all things, there are benefits and drawbacks to managing your property personally.

Benefits of personal management

The benefits of managing your property personally include:

❐ you may gain cost savings as no management fees will be deducted from your income

❐ you may be able to keep a closer watch on your property than a property manager does as you will probably have fewer properties to manage

❐ you can be sure that your own personal standards are upheld.

Drawbacks of personal management

The drawbacks of managing your property personally include:

❐   once you start to accumulate more and more properties, you may not have the time to manage all of them, especially if you are also employed or have other responsibilities

❐   you may lack full understanding of the laws applying to landlords and tenants and so strike trouble at some point

❐   the savings in costs may not be worth the cost of your time

❐   interviewing tenants and uncovering their financial and rental histories may be difficult.

In reality, the costs of professional management may be a small price to pay when you place a true value on the time you may spend yourself. Remember also that property management fees are tax deductible, which generally reduces them to a very small percentage of your income.

Managed by a property manager

Most real estate agents today will have a property management department of some description. Some property management companies are involved solely in property management. The success of this department or company can be measured not by the number of properties on its rent roll but by the percentage of vacancies it has, and the turnover of its tenants. Where turnover is high, this may be because of the nature of the particular area, or it could be due to the ineptitude or carelessness of the manager in selecting quality tenants.

Using a property manager also has certain benefits and drawbacks.

Benefits of using a property manager

The benefits of using a property manager include having an experienced manager who can:

❐   choose your tenant

❒ access credit information and rental histories of applicants

❒ carry out frequent inspections

❒ access a pool of tenants.

Drawbacks of using a property manager

The drawbacks of using a property manager are as follows:

❒ Paying a property manager can be costly as there are lots of hidden costs such as inspection fees, letting fees, advertising costs and sundries, all of which will add to the standard percentage cost of management.

❒ Property managers can be overworked—a single property manager can feasibly handle up to 50 properties alone. The manager you choose may have more properties than he or she can handle.

❒ Property management offices or companies can be staffed by inexperienced people or juniors who lack the skills needed to manage conflict or other issues, or think laterally to get your property tenanted in times of low occupancy.

If you are choosing to have your property managed by a property manager, you must be sure to take the time required to choose what you hope will be an efficient manager. Don't make the mistake of choosing a manager and then forgetting about your property, or simply opting for the management department of the agency which sold you the property. Be sure to keep a close eye on them so that they continue to do a good job for you.

If you are choosing to have your property managed, you must be sure to take the time required to choose what you hope will be an efficient manager

I recently had a period of vacancy in my unit in Queensland. The manager had told me that the existing tenants were coming to the end of the letting period, and as I am so busy these days I did not think to call and see if a new tenant had been found—I just assumed that she would call me if she was having any troubles.

About four weeks after the old tenant left, I called to ask about the situation, only to be advised that the property was still vacant and that the manager had been doing all she could to find a new tenant (at my expense, I might add). "Have you dropped the rent?" I enquired, knowing that the cash flow was enough to allow me some room to move. "Oh no," she said, "my landlords don't like to do that." I quickly made her understand that this landlord does like to do that and that she should have consulted me before making this decision on my behalf. I suggested that she try advertising a 12-month lease with a 6-month discount of $15 a week. You would have thought I was asking her to go to the dentist and have all of her teeth pulled, judging by her reaction! She simply did not want to reduce the rent at all and she could not see how losing $230 a week by having no tenant was equal to 15 weeks at the reduced rent. Well, of course I won, and we had a tenant within the next 48 hours. This tenant has since moved out and we are back to the $230 a week rent.

A property manager must do more than simply act as caretaker for you. If you are not happy with the manager you have now, get another one—and another one if you are not happy with him or her. It is very easy to cancel a property management agreement, and it is your job to oversee your manager to ensure he or she is doing the best job possible for you.

Management agreements

As outlined in previous chapters, many niche market properties come with an on-site manager already in place, who may have been retained under a range of different arrangements.

A management agreement refers to a written contract between the owner(s) of property (often as a body corporate) and an experienced operator. It will consist of a list of requirements of this manager, along with a schedule of remuneration for his or her services, typically expressed as a percentage of gross or net revenue.

Be very careful that when you read this agreement (which will usually be in place on a property before any of the properties are purchased and so available for review as part of purchase documents) all associated expenses are contained within, or at least included in, the expressed percentage management fee. Too often investors are told about the management fee but not informed about any associated expenses, which can sometimes push a 10 per cent management fee up to 30 or 40 per cent of the profits. Further, some of these expenses are fixed and do not depend on how much income you make.

Where a manager has been retained via a management agreement, and there is no associated granting of real estate or retail rights, it is usually fairly simple to terminate his or her services if the grounds are just. Ensure that you are familiar with the exit clause (and that there is one) and that there is not a large cost to terminate a poorly performing manager.

Management rights

Management rights are very similar to management agreements in their terms; however, management rights are usually 'purchased' by the manager and involve the acquisition of some of the real estate. Typically, management rights will be sold by the developer for several million dollars and may include an apartment in the complex plus rights over any restaurant, bar and reception area. Terminating a poorly performing manager who has purchased these rights can be fraught with problems, and very often these types of management rights are bought by couples with little or no hotel management experience. As outlined in Chapter 3, be very sure that you know as much as you can about the owners of these rights before you purchase— this is just as important as the forecast return of a property, as their performance will directly impact on your return, and can turn a potentially profitable investment into a disastrous one.

Leasebacks

Leasebacks differ from other management agreements in that they involve a manager actually signing a lease with each individual owner. Some investors feel more comfortable with this type of arrangement because it means that rent is going to be received even when there is no one occupying the property. This can be false security as, in reality, the ability of the manager to pay the lease is linked directly to his or her success in running a profitable venture. Where the venture returns less than needed to honour the lease agreements, the manager has to provide top up funds from other sources (such as the restaurant and bar that are a part of the complex your property is in, or even another establishment) or, if there is no other source, the lease will not be honoured. This has occurred often in recent times—close to where I live a large, well-known hotel operator liquidated quite suddenly leaving investors who thought they had a sound investment confused and unsure of what to do next. The liquidator was equally incapable of managing this well for the investors, and the story is still to come to a conclusion. Events like this leave investors holding an investment for which they can realise no immediate return, and which they have difficulty on-selling due to the unsuccessful history of the property.

Combination management

While the above examples of management arrangements may seem pretty straightforward, the reality is that, in practice, the arrangement attached to the property you ultimately buy may be a little bit of everything, and not quite so clear cut. Sometimes, there may be an income pooling arrangement, where all of the income made from all of the properties in any one complex collectively is placed into a pool and then shared fairly amongst all owners according to their share of the pool (most commonly determined by the size of each property). Yet other arrangements involve a fund put in place at the beginning of a predetermined period, usually the time considered reasonable for the venture to take off, which allows for individual investor returns to be 'topped up' in the event that a certain benchmark is not achieved.

The questions you should ask

Whatever the arrangement which is available on the property you are considering, even if it is one of a standard residential lease arrangement through a local real estate agent, there are questions you should be asking before you proceed with any manager. These include:

- ❒ How many properties do you currently manage, and what number of staff do you have to manage them?

- ❒ How often are inspections carried out and what is the cost of these?

- ❒ What is the actual percentage of the management fee, including all sundries, postage, telephone, leasing costs, advertising, letting fees, linen, laundry, cleaning and maintenance?

- ❒ How often are disbursements to the owner made? (While a minimum of monthly is most desirable, especially where you have borrowed to invest and must make regular mortgage repayments, don't be afraid to ask for fortnightly disbursements.)

- ❒ What action does the manager take when a tenant is behind in rent?

- ❒ How does a manager monitor tenant care of the premises?

- ❒ Has the manager any past cases of complaints from owners?

- ❒ What is the vacancy rate across the manager's rent roll or apartments in any one complex or resort?

- ❒ Has the manager experienced any past financial difficulty?

- ❒ Has the manager been involved in any failed companies or ventures?

- ❒ What strategy would the manager use to seek a tenant if your property experienced vacancy?

- ❒ What plans does the manager have to attract tenants to your property?

- ❒ What plans are in place for staff to manage the job when the manager takes annual leave?

- ❒ How many tenants on the books are currently in arrears?

❏ How many cases of serious tenant damage have been experienced in the past?

❏ What process does the manager use to screen tenants?

❏ In the case of a strata titled complex which is holiday let and managed on-site, does the body corporate have control over payment of some of the larger expenses?

❏ Is there a guard in place against secret commissions and undisclosed mark-ups? (These can occur where a manager uses 'mates' to perform work and receives kickbacks for selecting them.)

❏ Does the on-site manager have a business plan of how he or she will operate this business?

❏ What is the personal and/or business background of the on-site manager?

❏ Is the manager using a fair system of rotation for allocating apartments for occupancy?

You will probably think of more questions you can ask. When you retain a manager for the job of managing your property, the process should be taken seriously and treated in the same way as you would to recruit someone for any job. If and when the performance slips, waste no time in putting in place an action plan for the improved performance of the manager, or for his or her replacement in the event that this can fairly easily be achieved.

Some of your landlord responsibilities can be passed onto the entity you select to manage your property, while others remain with you

Landlord's rights and responsibilities

As a landlord, you have a number of responsibilities. Some of these are passed onto the entity you select to manage your property, while others remain with you. Following is a number of the responsibilities which you may find yourself charged with.

The agreement

It is the responsibility of the landlord to provide a tenancy agreement which satisfies the laws of the state in which he or she lives. While each state has its own laws, implemented through some form of Residential Tenancies Act, generally speaking certain requirements will be standard across the country.

A tenancy agreement can be written or verbal. Most written agreements will be made on a standard lease form or a Tenancy Agreement. The landlord may add clauses to this agreement, but not if they are contrary to the law. Where a lease agreement is verbal, the requirements of the residential tenancy act of that state still apply.

It is a requirement that the tenant be given an unsigned copy of any lease agreement prior to entering into the lease, for review and possible amendment. The landlord must also provide a copy of the signed agreement to the tenant within 14 days of it being signed.

Refusing a tenant

A landlord must consider all reasonable requests for tenancy from all applicants. There are harsh penalties for discrimination, and the unconscionable conduct and misleading and deceptive conduct provisions of the Trade Practices Act apply to landlords and their actions. Landlords can make a request that a tenant does not have pets within the property, but they are not allowed to refuse tenants with children unless:

❐ the landlord has been funded to provide accommodation for childless couples or people living by themselves

❐ the premises are the landlord's own home

❐ the premises aren't suitable for children (or are otherwise unsafe) because of their design or location.

Deposits

A landlord can accept a deposit from a prospective tenant, but this must be refunded when the tenancy agreement is signed, or

14 days after the tenant decides not to proceed with the tenancy. A 'holding' deposit designed to keep premises free while the tenants make up their minds is not legal, however. A landlord may not charge for preparing a residential lease or for entering into an agreement with a tenant.

Other monies to be paid

A landlord may ask a tenant to pay a bond, which provides funds for any repair work which may need to be carried out at the end of the tenancy. This repair work does not include items which are considered to be part of fair wear and tear, which the landlord must pay for. The landlord may not keep this money—it must be held in a trust account. Most states have rental bond boards which can provide these trustee services. This bond must be refunded within 7 to 14 days of the tenant's request to have it refunded, which can only be made after the tenancy period has expired. The bond can be any amount, but is not usually any more than four weeks rent where the rent is less than $200 a week ($300 in some states). Before charging a bond, a landlord must provide two copies of a condition report to the tenants and allow them a fair period of time (usually 48 hours) to inspect the property and advise of any damage not contained within that report. The fee for having this condition report prepared is paid by the landlord.

In some states, a landlord may also seek a letting fee, which is a contribution from the tenant towards the costs of obtaining the tenant. This usually cannot exceed one week's rent.

Receipts

It is the landlord's responsibility to ensure that a receipt is provided to the tenant for the bond. This receipt must be signed by the person taking the bond, describe what the money is for, state the amount, identify the account into which the money is going and provide other details such as the date and the names of all parties.

Collecting rent

Where rent is due to be paid weekly, a landlord may not ask for any more than two weeks rent in advance. Where the rent is due less than weekly, the maximum amount of rent in advance which can be sought is one month. The receipts required for rent have similar details to bond receipts.

Rent increases cannot be imposed until six months after a tenancy starts. Once rent has been increased, it cannot be increased again for another six months and 60 days' notice of rent increases must be provided to the tenant in writing.

Other responsibilities

The landlord must keep the premises in good repair at all times, and attend to all urgent repairs immediately. These include hot water service or electricity breakdowns, glass breakage, and events which cause danger to the tenants. Non-urgent repairs, such as minor building defects or appliance failure, must be attended to within 14 days of written notice being received. The landlord must make sure that all doors and windows have locks or can be secured in some other way. The landlord must give the tenant a key immediately upon changing any locks, and may not unnecessarily disturb the tenant or harass them in any way.

Moving in

The premises must be clean and in good order prior to a tenant moving in. Any metered electricity where there will not be a separate bill for the tenant must have the meter read on the day the tenant moves in.

The landlord must give no less than 7 and no more than 14 days notice of an impending inspection. However, in some states only 24 hours notice needs to be given for entry to value a property or show to prospective buyers, providing the entry is made within business hours. Under these circumstances, the landlord may not enter in an unreasonable way or stay longer than is necessary.

Moving out

Just because a lease has expired does not mean that the tenancy has come to an end. A tenancy does not end until a landlord (or his agent) has provided a valid notice that the tenancy is at an end.

After the lease has expired and the tenant chooses to vacate the premises, the landlord must have the premises inspected (usually done by the managing agent) and return the bond within a set period of time (different in each state). Bond monies cannot be unreasonably withheld and usually can only be used to cover damage left by the tenant which is not considered part of normal wear and tear.

Tenants' rights and responsibilities

A tenant has the right to quiet enjoyment of a property without being harassed by the owner. Too frequent visits or persistent phone calls by the owner may constitute harassment. Under these circumstances, a tenant may present the landlord with a 'Giving notice for breach of duty to landlord of rented premises from your tenant' notice. In a nutshell, this gives you, the landlord, 14 days to stop the behaviour or the tenants can take out an order against you forcing you to leave them alone.

Looking after the premises

Your tenants have to be sure that they maintain the premises in the order in which they found them. As a landlord, you must make allowances for normal wear and tear, but damage must be paid for by the tenants, either from their pocket or from their bond money, if it is discovered at the end of the tenancy. The tenants must notify you as soon as any damage has occurred and remedy the situation as soon as possible. They must also avoid becoming a nuisance and harassing neighbours.

If the landlord does not carry out repairs when requested, the tenants cannot stop paying rent. They can, however, have a notice issued and ask that the rent be paid into a special account, rather than to the owner, until the repairs are carried out.

When a tenancy agreement is coming to an end, tenants cannot stop paying the rent in deference to the bond being held. Tenants must pay rent up until the last day and then apply to have their bond refunded.

Electricity, phone, rates and water

While tenants will pay for their own electricity and telephone charges, water and council rates are paid by the landlord. In some states the landlord must also foot the bill for excess water charges, although in other states this is the responsibility of the tenant.

Other parties

Your tenant must advise you who will be living in the property and may not bring in additional or different people unless you agree to this. Your approval cannot be unduly withheld.

Ending a tenancy

If the tenant wishes to leave

In most states, a tenant can no longer break a lease, even when a good reason is given, unless the landlord agrees to the lease being broken. Where tenants wish to move out prior to the end of a lease, it is their responsibility to continue to pay the rent to the owner until a new tenant can be found. In many states, the tenants must also meet the costs of advertising for a new tenant.

Where tenants plan not to renew a lease, notice must be given to the landlord. The amount of time needed to give notice depends on the reason for ending the tenancy, but is generally 14 to 28 days.

If the tenants simply walk out, they are in breach of contract and the landlord can claim compensation for any money lost as a result. This is where landlord's insurance may come in handy.

If tenants can demonstrate that financial hardship will occur if they are forced to complete their lease, they may apply to the tribunal for the lease to be shortened, and this request may be granted.

If the landlord wants the tenant to leave

A landlord may not ask a tenant to leave prior to the expiration of a lease unless the tenant has in some way breached the lease agreement. Even in that event, the landlord may not physically throw out tenants or force them to leave in any other way.

If tenants dispute the reason for the ending of a tenancy agreement other than its natural expiration, they may apply to the tribunal for an extension of time to move, or to stay in the premises.

Where a legal notice has been served on a tenant to vacate a property and that notice runs out but the tenant is still in residence, the landlord may apply for a possession order. Even if this possession order is granted, the landlord still cannot use force to make the tenant leave. The police must enforce the order after the landlord gets a warrant of possession.

Goods left behind

A landlord may not keep any goods left behind as payment of unpaid rent or to offset any damage that has occurred. The landlord must make every attempt to contact the tenant and advise that the goods are available for collection. Each state has special rules for disposal of tenants' unwanted goods which are not subsequently collected by the tenant.

Serving of notices

All notices must be legally served upon the tenant or landlord. This can be done by:

☐ certified mail directly to the receiving party

☐ given personally to the person receiving it

❑ given to an employee at the agent's office (where management is handled by a property manager) or to an authorised person at the registered corporate office of the landlord in the event that the landlord is a company.

What to do in the event of a problem

No doubt you have read the latest story of the hapless investor who either had a one and only property investment severely damaged by hoodlum tenants, or was unable to evict non-paying tenants who appear to have been protected by some archaic law. For every one story of distress you may have read, I can guarantee to come up with 200 or more stories of landlord success and tenant heaven. The reality is, in your investing lifetime, you are unlikely to come across an event which cannot be managed towards a satisfactory outcome. However, if you do, there is help available.

You should always start by trying to solve any problems calmly through a dispute resolution process. See if both sides can come to some sort of agreement which can lessen the stress you may all be feeling.

If the dispute becomes too difficult for you, there is help available through your state or territory Office of Fair Trading, and through rental tenancy agencies and tribunals. These tribunals can deal with any dispute which involves a tenancy agreement and will act on your case if all other avenues have been exhausted. Where your case has resulted in extreme hardship, you can ask for it to be fast-tracked and dealt with as a matter of urgency.

Where a hearing results, the party who wins the hearing will have its costs paid by the other party. Where you are unhappy with the outcome of a hearing because you believe the hearing process was unfair, or that the tribunal made a decision it did not have the power to make, then you can take the matter to the Supreme Court.

Landlord's insurance

All owners of investment property should ensure that they are adequately insured. While most insurance companies do provide insurance for investment properties, there is only a small handful who provide landlord's insurance.

Landlord's insurance should, as a minimum, include:

☐ building and contents

☐ public liability

☐ loss of rent (through damage)

☐ recovery of unpaid rent

☐ tenant damage.

Be sure to thoroughly check the inclusions of any policy you may be considering. Many property managers offer an option to take out landlord's insurance for a nominal sum of around $5 a week. Be sure you do not simply accept this option because it is easy, and thoroughly research the cover to ensure it has all the necessary inclusions.

Summary

☐ Choosing to manage your property personally may save you a small amount of dollars, but may bring you troubles you don't need.

☐ Finding a good property manager can be difficult and is a task which needs to be taken seriously.

☐ Don't set and forget—watch the manager, review his or her performance and dismiss a poorly performing manager if necessary.

☐ Be sure you understand the arrangement which is in place for your niche market property or any property with an on-site manager.

❏ As a landlord you have responsibilities, the liablity for which cannot be passed onto your property manager. Be sure you are familiar with your responsibilities by visiting your state's Office of Fair Trading website.

❏ Landlord's insurance is a vital tool for damage control and compensation.

Conclusion

More often than not, the proud new owners of an investment property will simply hand the property management over to the agency from which they bought the property in the first place. Doing so usually means that the owner has not taken the time to thoroughly research the market and ensure the property manager chosen has the skills and experience to deal with any of the problems outlined in this chapter.

Make a detailed list for yourself of the skills you need in your property manager, and ask potential applicants to demonstrate their ability to deal with these issues. Be sure that they have had experience in the past and can detail for you actual situations they may have come across and how they managed them.

Be aware of the laws protecting you and your tenant in the state where your property is situated. Taking responsibility in this way may well head off any trouble before it has the chance to strike.

8   What happens in real life?

It doesn't matter how many books you read or how many courses you attend, you simply cannot beat real life experience as a learning tool. When I was a training instructor, I made sure that each and every training session I conducted included case studies involving real life events. This way, trainees could apply their learning immediately, at the time that it was most fresh in their minds.

Over the past 18 months I have received many reader questions, covering a multitude of topics and where possible I have replied with answers to these problems, providing my views on the best pathway to take. In this chapter, I would like to share with you some of the more common questions I have been asked and my answers, in the hope that you will learn more from this application of my strategies than I can teach you with a book full of information. In some of these questions some identifying details have been changed, while others may be a combination of several questions all seeking the same responses.

In your opinion, is it better to buy older homes cheaply in an up and coming suburb which has a fairly low capital growth at the moment, for, say, $75,000, or buy a property built after 1985 in a higher growth suburb for $125,000? There seem to be so many options available today that I have become confused—should I go for the bargain that will improve over the next few years, or the property which gives me tax benefits that I could write-off against my other income?

In asking whether you should go with the bargain which will improve over time, you're making assumptions about potential future capital gains which are based purely on your emotions or on what's happened in the past. Many an 'up and coming' suburb 'up and went' with little gain to be seen! The questions you should ask about both properties should start with the facts as you can establish them. What is the net position for each of these properties in terms of your own financial position? For the older property, does the rent return cover all of your costs and still give you an after-tax profit? Does the home built after 1985 give you a positive cash flow? If one of the properties turns out to be negatively geared, it could be that this will eliminate one of the choices.

If you find that both will have a positive cash flow, you must look at which one you'll qualify for, and this depends on the loan you need and how much equity you have in existing property.

If you're still left with two choices, find out the vacancy situation in the areas and if there are many similar houses being built in the area (which may flood the market with vacancies). Then look at other factors such as suitability as a rental and whether the properties can stand up to what may be hard wear and tear. Find out what your tenant market would be like—will the market for the type of property be people who are unlikely to default on rent, or is there a history of tenant damage and rent default in that area?

By this time you will probably be left with one clear choice. Note that none of these questions have anything to do with how you feel emotionally about the property (that is, its physical appeal) or on any assumptions you have made about the future.

We've recently had a property we bought not long ago revalued as we would like to expand our portfolio as soon as possible. We purchased the property 12 months ago and because of a recent development in the area that was sold at less than we paid, the valuation came just under the purchase price. This does not bother us too much as we intend to keep the property for a long time and at the moment we are looking to refinance. When the property was purchased, our deposit fell short of the minimum 20 per cent which the bank required to allow for an interest-only loan so we went with a principal and interest loan, intending to refinance shortly afterwards. Now we have saved another deposit for another property and since the value of this first property has not improved, I'm trying to decide if I should keep the loan on this first property at principal and interest or go for a fixed-term interest-only loan. Can you offer any insights here?

There are many people today who continue to sell the concept of acquiring interest-only loans to buy property as an investment. As a marketing tool, this is one way they convince people that they should go ahead with the purchase—since interest-only payments make it seem like the repayments are smaller, and less money is to be paid out of rent received on a property. The problem with this is it ignores the fact that all people have differing financial circumstances and so each person must have a borrowing strategy which suits them personally.

When you commence an investment portfolio, your aim should be to leverage against the growing equity in that portfolio to buy more property. Capital growth is not the only way that we can gain that equity, however. If we reduce the outstanding debt of the portfolio, we increase the amount of equity in that property and so leverage becomes possible.

This all means that we should be trying to minimise our investment debt by using rapid mortgage reduction principles (such as, a line of credit with all income sitting in the loan for as long as you can before drawing back), making principal and interest repayments, and ensuring that you obtain cash flow positive property which will give you extra money to pay into your debt.

The only time that you would not do this is when you still have a debt on the house in which you live (that is, non-tax-deductible debt). If this is the case, you should be using mortgage reduction principles on your own home debt, while your investment loans receive interest-only repayments. The moment your home debt is finalised, start making principal and interest repayments on your investment debt.

My husband and I have just paid off our house, which is valued at around $300,000. We have a substantial and diversified superannuation fund including shares and managed funds, to which we have contributed for many years. However, after September 11 we've been watching our superannuation funds going progressively backwards, and the principal sum has reduced quite markedly in a short period of time. We're a little nervous about investing in additional paper funds and want to invest in property. We'd very much like to invest in property in a popular resort town—there can be high rental return (for example, 10 per cent) but high costs as well due to the nature of the tenants, being short term, such as cleaning and electricity. In addition, there seems to be little or no capital gain historically—certainly this area has not moved much in the past ten years from a values point of view. Is this type of property a good idea or should we stick to capital cities where the growth is almost guaranteed?

I am a believer that astute investors should look past the capital gain issue alone and begin to consider a host of other important features when choosing an investment property. It's all very nice to have great capital gain but these days the rent return from property in capital cities is disproportionate to the purchase price—meaning you have to pay out a substantial amount of money each week just to cover the shortfall between the rent return and your costs. I am also very worried when I hear people talk of guaranteed capital gain—there are certainly many capital city investors who are relatively new to the market and who have found their market timing less than impeccable.

Some people may be prepared to take a low rent return and so have a large commitment from their own pocket while they wait for the next boom in the hope that eventually the gain will make it all worthwhile, but there's only so much money we can afford to contribute, and only so many of these kinds of properties we can afford. And then what happens if you don't get that expected growth after all?

You must work out the cash flow for any property. If this resort town property has a solid rental history and the rent covers all the costs and gives you money left over each week, then you can use this money to pay down any debt. This way, you'll still get the equity you need to leverage into more property and, since you're paying nothing out of your own pocket, you won't be so limited in the number of properties you can buy. And you never know— you have just as much chance of this town taking off as any other, especially if the past few years have been quiet on the gain front. Most towns have their day and you might just win on all fronts!

There seems to be a lot of hype around today advising investors to seek out only property which has been built in the last 15 years or so. Am I correct in assuming that the only way to achieve positive cash flow is from a building constructed after 1985?

Positive cash flow can be achieved on a property that looks like a negative cash flow one if it has enough on-paper deductions to make up all of the negative cash flow and more. So if expenses exceed income, it may be that on-paper deductions get back more than enough tax to make up the shortfall. Since 1985 was the first time that on-paper deductions for residential property were allowed, it's likely that only properties built after this time will fit into this category.

Of course, you can still get a positive cash flow if the income exceeds the expenses even without on-paper deductions.

However, we call this positive gearing as you'll make a gain and pay tax instead of making an on-paper loss and getting tax back.

If the property has income exceeding expenses *and* on-paper deductions, you may get enough on-paper deductions to actually wipe out the gain (on-paper only) so it looks like a loss after all, on which you will get tax back.

I desperately need some help to decide what I need to do with my first investment property. After doing a lot of research, saving up a nice deposit, getting good finance, finding the right place and buying it, I have run the figures through an investment calculator and it seems I'll be in the red for around nine years. Any ideas on how to turn the cash flow the other way—back towards the black, so to speak—or have I done something wrong?

Well, I wouldn't say you have done anything more wrong than the average investor. I suggest that perhaps at the point of purchase you did what many investors do—you looked at the property, felt 'good' about it and bought it because you 'thought' it was a good investment. You say that using the investment calculator was the last thing you did—may I suggest that this should have been the first thing you did, and when it showed that you would be in the red for almost a decade, that this might have been a good time to perhaps look at alternative property.

You cannot magically turn a negatively geared property into a positive cash flow one. However, do be sure that you have considered all things. If the property was constructed after 1985, have a good quantity surveyor inspect the property and provide you with a complete schedule of depreciable items. These on-paper deductions, if you haven't already considered them, can turn a negative into a positive in some cases. Often there's much more to claim than you may realise. Even a property built prior to this date may have various improvements which qualify for deductions.

Once this is all done, if you're still in the red, you probably need to get out there and find a property with enough positive cash flow to make up for this loss.

We seem to have come to a bit of a stalemate with our property portfolio, and we are not sure what the next steps should be. For family reasons we decided to sell up in Melbourne and with the proceeds we purchased two blocks of land in a large regional area. We built two very nice project homes on these blocks, one in which we live and one which is rented out. The capital growth has been significant, not only in the area itself, but because we were able to build these houses as owner builders, and so keep the costs down, making an on-paper profit as soon as we moved in.

The property which we have rented out, despite its low cost to build and rise in value, is not positive cash flow. Would it be better for us to sell the properties and using the capital gain we have made (a total of around $300,000) take it to invest elsewhere (and build another house for us) or hang onto them knowing that they are negatively geared but in a high growth area? If we sell, we will buy lower end property, still in growth areas, but perhaps with more chance of a positive cash flow.

Firstly, you must understand the difference between positive cash flow and positive gearing. Positively geared property is property where the rent return alone is more than the costs, and you pay tax on the difference. Positive cash flow is where the rent return plus the tax you now don't pay, due to on-paper costs such as depreciation and special building write-off, is more than the costs and the difference is after tax profit.

Then you need to see that you may be making some dangerous assumptions here—firstly, that the area you are now in, which has seen good growth already, will continue to grow, and secondly, that you will be able to choose another good growth area, as if there is some sort of crystal ball which will help you to predict this.

To answer your question fully, I would need to know how you have calculated that the property is not positive cash flow. As it is a new property which has already gained greatly in value (with most probably a rent increase following this growth) you must have a substantial amount of on-paper deductions, and since only the portion of any debt you have which relates to the one property can be claimed against your tax, I would be surprised if this property was not in fact a positive cash flow property.

If you have substantial equity in both properties together, you may be better to simply leverage against it. This way, you can still keep the existing properties, buy some more (subject to bank lending criteria, of course) with a 100 per cent loan (being sure that they are positive cash flow, even at 100 per cent) and so have several properties, all delivering more capital gain for you! Being sure that the new properties are positive cash flow will mean that you have no commitment from your own pocket.

You should also consider the fact that selling the properties would cost you money in sales commissions and so lessen your profits. In addition you'll pay capital gains tax on half of these profits, at your highest marginal rate of tax, whereas leveraging against them still allows you to take advantage of the capital gain you have enjoyed, without the costs.

We made the last repayment on our home loan a few months ago and now, after seeing so many of our friends take the plunge, feel ready to start an investment portfolio. The house we live in is valued at about $240,000. We have been in this house for 15 years and love it, although we would like to live a little closer to the beach. We have seen a house we like with a price tag of $280,000. Although we are a little nervous about raising another debt again, we will own quite a lot across both properties if we move out of our existing home and rent it out, and then use both properties to secure this new mortgage. The rent payments should help us with the new mortgage for the house we move into. Does this all sound like a good plan, and will the tax department let us claim some of the interest on the new loan, since it is partly secured by what will become an investment property?

Whoa! Slow down. You are possibly about to step into three very large mistakes, which I would like to outline one at a time before I provide you with a strategy which should be more financially sound for you.

1   Are you investing in property because your friends are, or because you truly want to? Be sure that this strategy is right for you, not just something you are doing to keep up with the Joneses.

2   If you love the house you live in so much, why are you moving out of it? Have you thought about how hard it will be for you to watch as someone else doesn't treat your house the way you would treat it yourself?

3   Did you realise that you are about to raise a very large, non-tax-deductible debt on a house to live in, while the house you rent out is debt free and so highly positively geared you will lose up to half of your rental income to tax?

The tax department will not let you claim any of the interest on the new loan as a tax deduction as this loan is not being used to purchase an income-producing asset. The fact that it is secured by an income producing asset does not make it an allowable deduction—the purpose of the loan is what determines its tax deductibility and in your case the purpose will be to buy a house to live in.

Let's imagine that you get $260 a week for your existing home as a rent return. You have $40 in property costs and you will then pay tax of around $103 (at the highest marginal rate of tax) on the balance, leaving you with around $117 a week. Your new loan of $290,000 (purchase price plus costs) will cost you over $400 a week to repay. This means that you must come up with $283 out of your after tax income to have this new house. You will have property valued at $530,000, with a debt of $290,000.

Now, let's say you sold the existing property instead. After costs you would realise around $240,000. You have no capital gains tax as it was your primary place of residence all of the time you owned it. The new home will cost you $290,000 with purchasing costs, so you must borrow a further $50,000. This costs you around $80 a week to repay. You then borrow $260,000 to buy another property as an investment. Let's say that you manage to get a property which is $15 a week positive cash flow, after all costs and after you have claimed your tax deductions (I am assuming you buy a newer property and ensure it has positive cash flow, so there will be an on-paper loss which will earn a tax cut, and this extra money pays the shortfall between any income and expenses). This $15 a week goes toward your mortgage on the house you live in, either as an extra repayment, or to help with the $80 a week (making your commitment just $65 a week).

You still have a house worth $250,000 and one worth $280,000 (total of $530,000) but now instead of paying out $300 a week, you pay out only $65 a week. Granted, your debt position is slightly higher (at $310,000), but the extra $235 a week you have from this strategy will make a nice hole in that balance pretty quickly, and you have less to commit to in the event that times get a little tough for you.

We have recently purchased our first investment property. I earn $20,000 a year and my husband earns $42,000. This should remain so for about the next five years at least—except for a six-month period next year when I will be on maternity leave (unpaid). With these incomes remaining static, what are your thoughts on setting up ownership with the bank (tenants in common or joint tenants) and what percentages would you suggest for tenants in common.

This is a very common question and one which must be thought through very carefully. Firstly, it must be made clear that it's not the bank that you set up ownership with—the bank is only providing you with the loan and the structure of this loan depends on the structure you choose to go on the title at the time of purchase.

Prior to signing any purchase contracts, if there is more than one purchaser you must decide in whose name you will buy the property. If you choose joint tenancy, the income will be split equally between all tenants as will the tax deductions. You might do this where both parties earn similar incomes, and you expect this to continue. If one party earns a higher income, you may wish to purchase in that name only. You would need to be sure that this situation was expected to continue for the long term—

if you think the imbalance in income earning is likely to change at some time in the future, buying in one name only today may not continue to be the best strategy. Once set up, it can be difficult to change your arrangement in most states.

'Tenants in common' is usually a structure chosen to allow the parties to 'will' their portions of a property to whomever they choose. It also allows investors to choose an uneven split of ownership. However, if the ultimate proportions are chosen simply to avoid tax or gain some other benefit for the lower income earner, like a tax deductible trip to inspect the property, the tax department may disallow the claim anyway. In other words, a tenants in common structure with an unequal split of ownership would need to be chosen only where there is another, pre-existing unequal relationship between the parties which can be proven (see Chapter 5 for examples of this).

Once you choose the structure, the bank will have requirements as to borrowers on the debt and guarantors. Usually, this relates entirely to the names on the title. In your case, the property has already been purchased, so it may be too late to make any changes to this structure.

My husband and I are both 55 years old and while we would like to take care of our own retirement, we feel we have left things a little too late. We do own our own home but have no extra money left over as we still have a few children living at home with us. We both have stable employment. Is there anything we can do?

Have you ever heard the expression 'if you aim for the stars, you may at least hit the treetops'? For you, this means if you begin on an investment strategy now, while you may not achieve the big financial goals you would like, you will at least be better off than you would have been if you had done nothing.

It is time you unlocked the equity you have in your home and used it for wealth building. While you are both still employed you can probably achieve quite a lot over the next six to ten years. Let's face it, even if all you could achieve is an extra $10,000 a year in income (unencumbered property of just $200,000), you will be doing better than most.

Understand the true level of your risk once you own your own home (as you do now), which is explained in full in the 'Risk Management' chapter of *How to Create an Income for Life*, and take the plunge.

My financial adviser has told me that shares are better than property as over time they provide a better yield. What do you think about this?

Technically speaking, your financial adviser is probably right—historically, a basket of blue chip shares has provided a better return over time than a selection of blue chip property. But let us look at the issues here:

❐ A good majority of investors never actually buy the shares or property used in the measurement sample—meaning they buy shares or property which have probably behaved much differently to the sample.

❐ If the measurement periods are the same (that is between the same period of years), this may not be a fair comparison, since property and shares usually behave in opposing cycles. For all we know the measurement period was an up cycle for shares and a down cycle for property.

❐ The commodities being compared are vastly different in nature and it is a bit like comparing chalk to cheese.

❐ The comparison is historical only and not a prediction of the future.

❐ Even if it proved somehow to be a fair and equitable comparison and shares are the best investment, does this mean you should only invest in shares? Are shares even right for you, considering your own personal risk profile? Will you be able to sleep at night if you invested all of your cash in shares or borrowed against your home for a share portfolio?

Since the real return of any investment really should be weighted by its risk factor, you are far better off considering what class of asset is most comfortable for you and then doing all you can to maximise the effectiveness of your investing in that particular class. Of course, down the track you cannot look back and wish you had chosen the other path!

We purchased a property in 1989 for $164,000, moving out of this property in 1994 but keeping it as an investment. At the time we moved out this property was valued at $230,000 by the bank providing us the investment loan. We have now sold this property for $280,000 and so have made a gain of $50,000. I believe we will only have to pay the capital gains tax on half of the $50,000.

My question is how will the tax department know that the price of the house was valued at $230,000 and not $164,000, as the bank has told me they can't give me a copy of the valuation as it is for their records only.

Firstly, did you pay for this valuation? If so, it is yours and the bank must provide it to you upon your written request.

Secondly, we live in a self-assessing tax regime, which means that you tell the tax department what the value was and they accept this. When we submit tax returns, we are not required to attach the documentation which substantiates our claims, but we must keep these records for five years. If during the five years you are selected randomly for an audit, you will be required to produce evidence that the property was worth the $230,000. At this stage, if the bank has not already given you a copy of the valuation, you could make another request to them or tell them you will provide them as the contact for the tax office, and that they should expect to assist the tax office with their enquiries when they call. Barring all of this, you will need to retain the services of a licensed valuer or a quantity surveyor to provide an opinion on the value of the property at the time you moved out.

As for the capital gains tax, remember to estimate a cost base first, which means deducting all costs associated with the sale, and perhaps even substantiated costs of turning it into an investment property, from the gain before you halve it.

9 The odds and ends

- ❏ Debate still rages over capitalising investment loans
- ❏ You can remain within tax office rules when using rapid mortgage reduction on your investments
- ❏ There are many investment schemes to be wary of
- ❏ Buying on holidays can be a mistake
- ❏ Land tax is a manageable fact of investing
- ❏ Should you rent or buy?

And now we come to perhaps my favourite part of any book—the second last chapter. This is the chapter where all of those things which just did not seem to fit anywhere else are written. You probably have some unanswered questions at this stage and hopefully you will find that question answered in this chapter. If not, email them to me and I will be sure to include them in the next book (there is always a next book!).

Capitalising loans

Every time I write a new book, there is a new opinion to report as far as capitalising investment loans is concerned. When split loans first became popular many years ago, a clever property marketer developed a strategy which enabled investors to pay all the income from an investment property into the personal portion of their debt, or the debt for their owner-occupied property, while the interest accruing on the investment portion of the debt simply added up, making the debt larger and larger and thus increasing the tax deductions. While this was happening the home loan was, of course, reducing at a great rate of knots, making investors feel more and more secure as they watched their personal debt magically disappear. Some marketers went so far as to suggest that all costs, such as rates and body corporate fees, also be taken from the investment portion of the debt, effectively meaning that all rent was pure profit, and all property costs simply added to the loan balance along with the interest. I had a client at the time whose accountant suggested she even throw the cost of a car on top of the whole deal—claiming the interest on this part of the loan as a tax deduction as well!

Of course, the tax department didn't like any of this one little bit, and so a decision was made on a test case which disallowed a claim for capitalised interest. At this point, the tax department pointed out that it would be acceptable to pay only the interest bill on the investment portion of a split loan (that is, principal reductions did not need to be made), as long as the balance did not increase over time for anything other than a legitimate claimable cost, such as a renovation or repair.

In a landmark case in mid-2002 this decision was overturned, paving the way for investors to once again begin the process of capitalisation of their investment loans. The case is, as at the time of writing, under appeal and it is highly likely that the overturned decision will be reversed yet again.

So, where does this leave investors? Clearly, the tax department is unsure of what the final outcome will be. As an investor, you must make the decision yourself as to which is the better road for you to take. While I will agree that those people with large, non-tax-deductible home loan debt may benefit from keeping their investment debt on the increase (and so maintaining tax deductions longer) while they pay off their personal debt more quickly, I personally found it much easier to simply make interest-only repayments on my investment debt while I paid all of the extras, including my positive cash flow, into my personal debt.

Let us take a look at two examples to see what the differences would be between two investors. To make the comparison more simple, I will assume construction depreciation only, for a period of 40 years, and make all other things equal between the two examples. I will also consider the investment debt as the only cost, assuming for this illustration that both parties meet the property costs from personal income.

Nicholas and Elisabeth had a $150,000 mortgage on their own home, and a $250,000 investment debt, both at 6.8% interest. Their financial circumstances were as follows:

Income	$45,000 each
Rent return	$15,600
Depreciation	$5,000
Interest on investment debt (interest-only repayments)	$17,000 a year

They use the rent for this repayment and add $1,400 a year to this rent to cover the interest (provided by the positive cash flow).

Repayment on personal mortgage (paid fortnightly)	$16,000 a year

Nicholas and Elisabeth's personal mortgage would take 14.92 years to repay, after which we will assume that the $16,000 a year is paid as extra repayments to the investment debt (on top of the $17,000 being paid now, which we will assume is maintained even as the interest bill declines), finalising this debt in a further 10.65 years. In total, their debt repayment takes 25.57 years.

Elsa also had a $150,000 mortgage on her home, and a $250,000 investment debt, both at 6.8% interest. Her financial circumstances were as follows:

Income	$50,000
	(same tax bracket)
Rent return	$15,600
Depreciation	$5,000

Interest on investment debt starts at $1,416 in month one but increases as the debt grows if capitalisation is chosen. No repayments are made and debt increases.

Repayment on mortgage	$16,000 a year plus
(paid fortnightly)	$15,600 rent

To make a fair comparison, I will also assume that Elsa places an extra $1,400 a year, from the positive cash flow, into this mortgage until it is finalised.

Her personal mortgage would take 5.46 years to repay, after which her investment debt has grown to $360,955.46. We will assume that the $16,000 a year is paid as extra repayments to the investment debt (on top of $17,000 which is equivalent to the amount paid by Nicholas and Elisabeth), finalising this debt in a further 20 years. In total, debt repayment takes 25.46 years

Your individual circumstances will determine which one of these strategies is most beneficial for you, as will the actual cash flow on the properties which you choose for your portfolio. Before deciding on whether to capitalise your loans or not, do be sure that you seek expert advice on the best structure for your own personal circumstances. The free Destiny Finsoft Program (version 5 or above) can carry out these calculations for you.

Mortgage reduction for your investment loan

Recently I applied to the tax office for an individual ruling on a personal issue I had. My current loan is for investment purposes only, with my personal debt having been repaid in full some time ago. I wanted to use mortgage reduction principles to reduce the principal of this investment loan more rapidly. I had worked out that, if I placed all of my income into my investment loan and left it there as long as I could before I withdrew it to pay off my credit card and other expenses, I could minimise the interest bill dramatically and so repay the investment debt much more quickly, creating equity at a faster rate for leveraging purposes. As it turned out, the amount I 'drew back' for personal spending was considerably less than what I was going to 'leave in' as extra repayments, and since the tax department actually only required an interest-only repayment, I felt I was doing it a big favour. In fact, what I was doing was reducing my debt and so reducing the amount of tax I could claim back—in effect getting myself into a position where I would pay more tax as my properties moved towards being positively geared rather than positive cash flow.

So, I carefully explained the strategy in a three-page document, pointing out the benefits to not only myself (as in debt minimisation) but to the tax department as I became less of a burden and my tax payable increased. I also outlined how, as an alternative should this strategy not be acceptable, I would simply pay interest only on my investment loan and spend the extra money on myself (flippant, yes, but designed to get my point across).

You can imagine my shock (although I cannot say it was entirely unexpected) when the answer came. The tax department officer had carefully regurgitated my request (assuring me that it was clearly understood) and advised me that, no, sorry, I could not do this. If I chose to go ahead with this strategy, all of the money I paid in would be considered debt repayment, and all of the money that I took out would be considered drawings for personal use, thereby raising a personal debt once again while I accelerated the repayment of my investment debt. They were using their best efforts to discourage me from undertaking a strategy designed to lessen their commitment to me in the way of tax concessions, even though I was doing my best to reduce my dependency on this country. They did not seem able to see the benefits.

Under normal circumstances, I can fully appreciate that if you draw from an investment loan to pay for personal expenses, you should not be allowed to make a claim for the portion of the interest which relates to the amount you withdrew. In my case, however, I was actually lending the money, in effect, to my investment debt temporarily, so that this debt could benefit from interest offset. In addition, I was even going to leave enough in the account each month to continue to reduce the outstanding balance and so repay the debt. If I had ever wondered at the wisdom of a government department before, this episode signified the first time I was actually rendered speechless!

Hence, if you find yourself in the position of having only an investment debt, having finalised your personal mortgage, and you wish to utilise mortgage reduction principles to reduce this debt as quickly as you can, you must approach the task of debt repayment from the back door.

Firstly, ensure that you have the right loan. *How to Create an Income for Life* explains in detail the features of the most effective investment loan—which, most importantly, should be a line of credit with the ability to split for different purposes.

After ensuring this, split off, say, $10,000 of your investment debt into account number one, leaving the balance in account number two. Operate solely from account number one, placing all of your funds from income and rent into this account and drawing back for personal expenses. Pay and then claim only the interest on the portion of the debt you are not working on, that is the debt in account number two. Then, when the balance of account number one approaches zero (as it will whenever you use rapid mortgage reduction), drawback to the full $10,000 limit and make a lump sum payment to account number two, effectively making a lump sum payment off the principal. The penalty for using this method of debt repayment to you is that you will not be able to claim the interest on the $10,000 in account number one as a tax deduction without dramas from the tax office. This will not really matter as, in reality, if you were to calculate the actual cost to you of the interest on this small portion of the debt, which actually grows less each day as you practise rapid mortgage reduction, it is a small price to pay for staying on the right side of the tax office.

Schemes to be wary of

If I had $10 for each person who has ever approached me to tell me about a course he or she attended which has not come off as expected, I would be as rich as the presenters of those dubious get-rich-quick schemes. At the risk of becoming arch enemy number one to rags-to-riches icons who are revealing the secrets only the rich know to anyone with a spare $10,000 or more to spend on the tuition (what am I saying, I have been an enemy to these people for years now!) I want to issue another warning to anyone considering an investment in such a course without knowing exactly what they are going to get for their money.

> *Don't consider an investment in any course without knowing exactly what you are going to get for your money*

Don't do it! If I could name them, I would, but you know who they are. They have four-page colour spreads in national magazines about mastering this and that in just four short days. They have advertisements in the national press depicting themselves next to their fancy sports car as the spiel outlines how they skyrocketed from bankruptcy to multi-millionaire at the speed of light (don't you ever wonder, just for a millisecond, why they went bankrupt in the first place?). You see them exuberantly espousing little titbits of information at free (or very cheap) introductory sessions designed to coax you into taking the big step onto the major workshop with the five-figure price tag.

While indeed there are many reputable workshop presenters around, in some cases the strategies taught are at best risky and at worst dangerous, and they number in their hundreds. Recently, some good investigative journalism has uncovered some of the more unsavoury of practitioners who often present downright illegal strategies.

There are, however, other less obvious strategies that you should approach with caution, some of which are discussed below.

Purchasing multiple deposit bonds

In this scheme, multiple deposit bonds are used to buy off–the-plan apartments with long-dated settlements which are then to be sold just before settlement at extreme profit.

The best-case scenario here is that the investor has timed the market perfectly and manages to sell all of the purchases just prior to settlement for a profit. More common, though, is the investor who is left unable to sell these properties, forced to proceed (as there is a binding contract in place) or lose the deposit. The extent of the loss is not limited to the price of the bond (which is normally around 1 per cent of the purchase price) but includes the 10 per cent deposit, which is paid to the vendor by the underwriter of the bond who counter claims against the investor. There have even been cases where these investors have been charged with mortgage fraud for not disclosing to the banks they approached for finance approval (usually required before a bond can be issued) that they had other offers of finance also in the wings.

Where investors using this strategy decide to proceed with the purchase, it is usually highly unlikely that they will have the borrowing power (or the equity across all of the properties) to fund the purchase of all properties they have contracts on. This particular strategy becomes dangerous when a property lull is experienced, such as began in most capital cities at the end of 2002.

Bribing valuers or obtaining multiple valuations

After learning how to bribe valuers or obtain multiple valuations on a proposed property, investors in this scheme are advised to use the highest valuation to get the money for the purchase from the bank (on the assumption that the bank lends a percentage of the valuation) and the lowest valuation to haggle the price with the vendor. For example, one valuer tells you the value is $560,000, while another says $490,000. You negotiate the purchase price at $490,000 (based on the low valuation) while you borrow 90 per cent of the $560,000 ($504,000) to buy the property. You have now obtained 110 per cent finance with no money down, and you can further use the higher valuation to claim a higher value (and possible quick sale) on the property.

There are many problems with this strategy, the main one being that valuers have been under fire for these very practices, and banks are whittling down their panelled valuers to those they feel they can trust to deliver sound valuations. Add to this the fact that most banks lend on purchase price rather than valuation anyway and it is easy to see why this strategy is doomed to fail. Market price is whatever a person is willing to pay for a property, and banks lend on market price. In addition, valuers work on behalf of the bank, not the borrower, so any form of bribery or collaboration with a valuer is highly unlikely.

> *Market price is whatever a person is willing to pay for a property, and banks lend on market price*

Instantly increasing property values

I have to say I got a kick out of this one when I heard about it. The investor buys a four-bedroom house for $200,000, which is rented for $220 a week (0.11 per cent of the purchase price as a weekly rent return). He then rents it to four university students at $65 each a week, raising the rent to $260 and the value to $236,000 (based on the theory that rent return determines price, as outlined in Chapter 2). The investor then buys a car for $10,000, adds that to the property and adds $20 a person to the rent for the use of the car. This raises the rent to $340, and lifts the value of the property to $299,000 ($309,000 based on the $340 a week rent, less the value of the car). All in a day's work!

The problem with strategies like this is that they ignore the fact that even students will seek out property to rent at current market value. Over-inflating of rental prices in this way may lead to vacancies when you cannot find tenants who are willing to pay.

Seeking out distressed sales or deceased estates

This scheme involves haunting the obituaries and seeking out distressed sales or deceased estates, and then moving in and making ridiculous offers to the grieving family. This one can be taken one step further. The investor buys a property worth $200,000 for $160,000 at a distressed sale. He then immediately markets it for $200,000. The new buyer borrows 80 per cent ($160,000) and the investor lends the balance to the new owner ($40,000) at 12 per cent interest. This interest provides further cash flow to the investor for more investing. Deceased estates may offer fair bargains but they actually don't come up that often.

Schemes such as these take a large amount of time and effort, and often the properties purchased need a lot of additional work to make them re-saleable. In addition, any scheme which requires the vendor to finance a new borrower adds another level of risk to the transaction and requires much thought and research by the vendor. For most direct property investors who have busy lives and limited time, strategies such as these may complicate the investing process and make it all too hard.

Buying a run-down property and doing it up

The idea behind this strategy is to buy a run-down property and spend hundreds of hours of your time doing it up, selling the property again in three months for a $50,000 profit. I have never seen this one work at all—except on paper, where the personal time and effort of the investors is not given a true value. While most people believe that aesthetic appeal adds tens of thousands of dollars to the value, this is usually the exception rather than the norm. Substantial value is usually only added by complete renovation or additions to property, not from paint jobs or gardening.

These are just some of the dubious schemes which are storming the country and which will continue to do so while willing disciples flock to courses to learn about them. There are, of course, an abundance of legitimate workshops with fair price tags which can teach you an enormous amount of valuable information. In the end, it will be common sense, caution, hard work and patience which will pay off and ensure that you truly do have an income for life. Remember (haven't I said this before?), if it sounds too good to be true, it definitely is. There is no such thing as a free lunch. Life wasn't meant to be easy. And all that.

> *It will be common sense, caution, hard work and patience which will pay off and ensure that you truly do have an income for life*

Holidays

I have two things to say about holidays and although I say these two things in every book, I do feel they are important.

Firstly, please do not fall into the trap of buying an investment property while you are on holiday. Believe me, I know that relaxed and mellow feeling so well, and my own portfolio would be chock-a-block full of holiday apartments by the beach if my feet weren't so firmly planted on the ground. You cannot make a wise purchase decision after a few hours in the sun or straight after a massage.

And secondly, if a marketer includes as a feature of your potential purchase the chance of a tax-paid trip twice a year to inspect the property, ignore it. You cannot claim the costs of a holiday on your tax return if you also happen to inspect a property while you are there. If you fly to the area, look at the property and then fly home, you may be permitted to claim all of your costs. But, if you so much as dip your toe in the ocean, or stay the night when you really don't need to, the purpose of the trip becomes one of having a holiday and at best you can claim taxi fares to and from the actual property. And why should it be any other way?

Land tax

At a recent seminar an older gentleman came to me and told me he was giving up buying property because the land tax was killing him. While the land tax was a problem for him, at the end of the day he still made more money than he was making by not investing at all. It reminded me of the pensioners in the bank when I was a young teller—they had non-interest bearing accounts with hundreds of thousands of dollars in them because they knew they would lose 50 cents of pension for every dollar of interest they made. None of them seemed to realise they would still be 50 cents ahead of where they were from doing nothing, even after the loss of pension!

Land tax is a fact of life and a cost of investing. The thought of it should not be a reason to choose not to invest. Since land tax is levied on the land value of your properties, you can minimise land tax by realising that apartments and townhouses usually have a low land content in their values. You may be able to own many more units or flats before you become liable for land tax than you can own houses. In addition, land tax is a state tax. By spreading your investing around the country you can also minimise your land tax liabilities.

Buying away from home

Back to another favourite topic of mine. It seems no matter how passionate I become on the subject, there are still people I simply cannot convince to invest outside of the circle in which they live.

When we buy property, we tend to cast the net five kilometres around where we live and that is where we buy. Not only is this assuming that the area you live in is the best you can get for your investment dollar (which it may not be) but this strategy ignores the many good value, high potential properties you can find in areas other than your own, and in states other than your own.

If you are still uncomfortable about buying property you have not seen, read again the list of questions to ask in both this book and in *How to Create an Income for Life*. Once you have satisfactory answers to these questions and you have asked for photos of the property (if you really must have a bit of touchy-feely), ask yourself what more could you achieve by actually going there? All you will do is form an attachment which may make hard decisions even harder.

Recognise and appreciate that we have a large and wonderful country with hundreds and hundreds of unique investing opportunities hidden in every one of its four corners. Don't waste these opportunities by limiting yourself to only that tiny area in which you live.

> *We have a large and wonderful country with hundreds of unique investing opportunities hidden in every one of its four corners*

Rent or buy?

New investors who have not yet purchased a home in which to live may well ask whether it is better to invest first (renting a home in which to live) or buy a property to live in first.

This question requires a two part answer. The first part is that, on this occasion, your emotions may well come into the decision-making process. If you would like to have a place to hang your hat, so to speak, something you can paint however you choose and hang pictures to your heart's content, then buying an owner-occupied home may well be your first priority. Save as much deposit as you can, buy the home and pay off as much as you can quickly. As soon as you have a small amount of equity, leverage into an investment property. Remember that the price of your first (or second or third) property does not have to be high in order for it to be successful for you.

On the other hand, there may be an occasion where buying an investment property first may work out well, too. Clients of mine recently asked if they should keep saving the deposit to get the home they really wanted to live in (which would probably take another two years, due to the area in which they had chosen to buy), or use the deposit to buy a cheaper investment property now.

Presuming that these people were prepared to carry out the research to maximise their chances of investing success and were sure to buy positive cash flow property, it may well work out for them to use their deposit now to buy an investment property. This way, rather than keeping their deposit in a bank or other low-interest vehicle, they will be accessing potential capital gain by entering the property market now. In addition, the positive cash flow they may get would serve to accelerate the speed with which they continued to save. At the end of a one or two-year period, they would have as a deposit:

❐ the money they had saved up after the purchase from their incomes

❐ the additional funds they had saved up from the positive cash flow

❐ the increased value of the property they had purchased.

At this stage these clients would leverage from the investment property into a home of their own, using its increased value and their savings as a deposit.

The choice is a personal one; however, do be sure to work out the figures before making a decision either way.

Summary

❐ The responsibility for successful investing lies with you.

❐ If you are capitalising a loan, be sure this is the right strategy for you.

❐ Reduce your mortgage as quickly as possible, using arrangements within tax law.

❐ Beware of feeling mellow while on holiday and buying property which is not right for you.

❐ Be certain you know your land tax responsibilities and do your best to minimise them.

❑ Increase the success of your property investing by widening the circle from which you choose property to include the rest of the country.

Conclusion

The information you now have, combined with the vital financing, property and budgeting information which was provided to you in my first two property books, will bring you up to date on the latest tax information as at time of writing, and help to make your investing the success you should expect.

By taking responsibility in this way, by educating yourself, you have become ready to manage the challenge which comes with every property portfolio. The learning must never stop—each day something new will develop and there will be more to know and greater challenges to conquer. Look at the journey with the confidence that comes with newfound knowledge and go forth with wisdom and enthusiasm.

10　Onwards and upwards

You are probably reading this book because you have already commenced investing and would like to go forward armed with more in-depth knowledge. Or, perhaps you just want to be sure that you have every piece of information you need before you take the plunge and buy your first investment property. Either way, it is most likely that you have decided (or discovered) that it is very hard today to find one person who can tell you everything you need to know—yesterday! Every way you turn you discover some little piece of information which would have been useful to you.

For investors in any asset, the rules are the same as those in life. The person responsible for where you head, what you do and what you ultimately achieve, is you.

The world has changed in recent years. We have all learnt valuable lessons about life and hopefully have begun to realise that now, more than ever, we have to put our heads down and our tails up and make the most of the precious life we have, today. While we can never be sure that we will have a long-term future, we can know that we have the power in our hands to make a difference to our own lives and to those of the people we love.

The road for you will be littered with rocks and potholes, but it is a road no less and which road you take is your choice, and yours alone. Let's summarise the things you need to know in order to make your journey as smooth as possible.

You must understand that property will provide a different return for you than other asset classes, and that different types of property can be successful for you in different ways.

One way to make a return from property is through its capital growth. Another is through the cash flow today. As an investor you must learn how to read property returns and establish what the true return on any property investment really is. Knowing more about return and the ability of any one property purchase to deliver the returns you are seeking is an important first step for all property investors.

The debate between cash flow investors and growth investors will rage eternally. Growth investors will seek out blue chip property designed to deliver high capital growth. To achieve this they will willingly commit personal funds, at times experiencing lifestyle changes to do so. These investors may be rewarded by big gains in short periods of time. Many of them, however, may never get to these gains as the weekly commitments cripple them financially.

Cash flow investors believe that growth is secondary. Many cash flow investors may have a lifestyle today which they are not willing to compromise, or perhaps they simply cannot afford to invest at all unless there is positive cash flow to be seen. While cash flow investors may not realise such large gains as the growth investor, they usually experience less short-term pain and have more chance of being there for the pay off. Often cash flow investors happily discover that the gain is realised after all.

It's not for me to make a judgement over who is right and who is wrong. We must not spend time justifying our position, or otherwise believing that our strategies are better than another's. What is more important is that each investor fully understands each method of property investing and chooses a strategy which works for him or her both today and in the future.

Once you have put together a portfolio of properties, your work does not end. Each property investor must be sure that the effectiveness of his or her portfolio is managed on an ongoing basis. Monitor your properties individually and your portfolio as a whole to be sure that it continues to meet your goals today and in the future. Identify when a property has served its purpose and establish those properties which may need early liquidation. Be sure that eventual liquidation of your portfolio is managed to occur at a time most financially viable in terms of income and tax.

Don't be afraid to set an upper limit which sits comfortably for you in terms of price. You do not have to spend a large amount of money on each purchase to obtain properties which will perform well for you. More important is your own comfort and willingness to continue to increase the number of properties you hold.

Be aware of the important role that niche market property can play in your portfolio, but at the same time be certain you know its limitations and potential impact on your entire portfolio. While forecast returns may seem too good to pass up, they may come at the cost of increasing your portfolio if choosing a niche market property limits the number of properties you can acquire. Be certain that you can finance such a property without hardship.

Successful property investing will only occur where the choosing of property has been carried out diligently. All investors have a responsibility to themselves to ensure they carry out their own research and increase the chance of successful investing. Where investors experience difficulties after purchase, most often this is due to lack of effective research on the part of the investor. Know the questions to ask when buying any property and be sure they are asked of the right people. Explore the management arrangements and fully understand any agreements which may be attached to property you are considering. Refuse to purchase property which will not provide a positive cash flow to you from day one. Research the area you are looking to buy in and the future plans of council. Know the population movements and the extent of demand for rentals and sales. At all times maintain a commercial approach to your investing—there is no place for emotions in this process.

Become smarter than your accountant when it comes to accessing your tax benefits. Use the tax benefits to help you minimise debt as quickly as you can, so that slow capital gain will not impact so heavily on you. Remember that you are personally responsible for the preparation of your own tax return—even when you use a professional to assist you.

Be careful when you use any unusual or comprehensive purchasing structure. If your property investment involves a 'buy and hold' strategy, you cannot afford to put in place a structure which will not remain efficient for the term of your investment. Project ahead 10 or 20 years and do the sums to be sure that any unusual structure you choose continues to work for you. Be particularly careful when buying in single names, as joint tenants or tenants in common, and be familiar with the tax department allowances for these structures.

Just because you choose to have a professional agent manage your property does not absolve you of your responsibility as a landlord. You remain responsible at all times and severe penalties can be applied if you do not carry out these responsibilities with care. Know what the state in which your property is situated will require of you, by visiting Fair Trading and Real Estate Institute websites. Be sure that your landlord's insurance policy is adequate and current. On-site management takes particular care in the choosing and supervision so be sure to know as much about this management as you can before signing any contracts.

Be careful of undertaking any risky strategies which may be suggested at high price seminars or by rags-to-riches gurus. There really is no such thing as a free lunch and most of these strategies may well have a very steep downside.

Be sure to always work on debt minimisation, but where your loan is a line of credit beware of the traps of using rapid mortgage reduction. Capitalising your loan may also not be such an effective strategy for you so be sure you know the ultimate outcome before doing this.

In the end it is all pretty much common sense. Trust your own judgement and ask yourself whether you will still be able to sleep at night after you take on any potential strategy. As I mentioned earlier in the book, investing is really meant to be fun and invigorating. I have been encouraged by the great number of people all over Australia who write to me to advise me of their own investing success—everyday people like you and I who do not necessarily take great risks, but who commit to being sure that they take the responsibility for their own future firmly in their hands.

Good luck, have fun, enjoy the journey and reap the rewards!

Glossary

ASIC: Australian Securities and Investments Commission.

Body corporate: An owners' committee with owners volunteering for positions. In place to manage funds collected to maintain common property in strata titled properties.

Bond: An amount of money paid by the tenant and held in trust to cover any damage at the end of a rental period.

Borrower: A party to a loan—the person borrowing the funds.

Business plan: A document outlining the future plans of a business and projecting income and expenses for the planned period.

Capital costs: Costs incurred when purchasing a property as well as those paid for structural improvements.

Capitalising: Allowing the interest on a loan to build up without paying any repayments at all. The loan balance will increase.

Capital gain: The profit made on an investment.

Capital loss: The loss made on an investment.

Certificate of Title: Legal proof of ownership of a property, carrying the owner's name and other information.

Commission (real estate): Fee payable to a real estate agent (or other salesperson) for selling a property by the person authorising the sale. Usually a percentage of the sale price, or can be a set fee where a relationship between the developer and salesperson exists.

Common property: Areas in strata-titled properties shared and maintained by all owners.

Compound: The process whereby the value of an investment grows exponentially over time.

Contract of Sale: Written agreement setting out the terms and conditions of a property sale.

Conveyancing: Legal process of transferring the ownership of a property from one person to another. Can be carried out by either a property solicitor, a conveyancer or a settlement agent.

Deposit: Usually 5 to 10 per cent of the purchase price of a property placed in trust upon exchange or signing of the contract.

Deposit bond: An insurance policy guaranteeing a purchaser's deposit in the event of a contract default.

Depreciation: Where the original cost of an item is progressively written off over its effective life.

Developer: The person providing the funds (personal or borrowed) and taking the risk for building a property for sale.

Equity: The difference between what you owe and what you own of a property.

Fittings and fixtures: Items such as baths, stoves, lights and other fittings, kitchen, linen or storage cupboards or wardrobes. Fittings are not normally included in a contract if they can be removed without causing damage.

Forecast: Assumptions made (often on paper by developers) about the future growth and income earning potential of an investment, based on historical performance and projected future events.

Gross income: Income earned before tax and any costs.

Guarantor: A party to a loan who is not a borrower. A guarantor provides a guarantee for the debt to be paid in the event that the borrower defaults. Often a guarantor provides security for a debt for someone else.

Interest: The sum charged by the lender, calculated on the outstanding balance of borrowings, in deference to having supplied you with funds.

Interest-only loans: A loan on which interest only is paid periodically and the principal is paid at the end of the term.

Investment: The purchase of a security with the ultimate goal of producing capital gain or an income.

Joint tenants: Joint tenancy is the equal holding of property by two or more persons. When one party dies, the remaining tenants share the portion owned by the deceased.

Land tax: Value-based levy applied to some property. Varies from state to state.

Landlord: The owner of an investment property.

Lease: A document granting possession of a property for a given period without conferring ownership. The lease document specifies the terms and conditions of occupancy by the tenant.

Leverage: To utilise the growth in any one investment vehicle to invest into more vehicles.

Mortgage: Legal agreement on the terms and conditions of a loan for the purpose of buying real estate, whereby the person offering the mortgage takes security over property.

Negative gearing: The writing off of investment property losses where a negative cash flow results—that is, expenses exceed income.

Net income: In-hand income after tax and costs.

Net profit: Remaining funds left after all costs are paid.

Niche market property: Property which is zoned residential but provided for specific markets—such as tourism, retirement or student.

Occupancy: Period that a tenant occupies a property.

On-paper deductions: Tax claimable items which do not have a relative cash outlay.

On-site management: Care and letting of premises carried out by a manager who lives at the site.

Owner-occupied: Property in which the owners reside—that is, non-income-producing property.

Positive cash flow: The net positive income earned on a property after adding rent plus tax breaks and deducting actual property costs.

Positive gearing: Where income on an investment property exceeds expenses and tax must be paid on the gain.

Principal: The original amount of money that has been borrowed not considering accruing interest.

Real property: Land, with or without improvements.

Repayment: The amount required by a lender to repay a loan, including its interest, within a set period of time.

Revenue costs: Costs incurred to earn income on an investment property.

Risk profile: Outlines the level of risk an investor can stand according to questions they answer about how they feel about investing and their personal investing choices.

Security: Property offered to the mortgagee in return for a loan.

Settlement: Completion of sale (or advancing of a loan) when the balance of a contract price is paid to the vendor and the buyer is legally entitled to take possession of the property.

Shares: Unit of ownership in a publicly listed company, which can be traded on the stock exchange.

Special building write-off: The amount of depreciation which can be claimed on the construction costs of an investment property.

Stamp duty: A state government tax imposed on the sale of real estate.

Strata title: Most commonly used for flats and units, this title gives you ownership of a small piece of a larger property and includes common property.

Superannuation: A sum of money invested which by law cannot be accessed until the investor reaches 'preservation age'.

Tariff: The amount paid by a traveller for short-term accommodation.

Tax: An amount of money paid to the government as a percentage of each dollar earned.

Tax benefits: Any allowable item which reduces the amount of tax you must pay.

Taxable income: Income on which tax is paid after allowable deductions have been considered.

Tenancy in common: The holding of property by two or more persons, with either equal shares or unequal shares. If one person dies, the property is dealt with in accordance with the will.

Tenant: Either the person signing a lease to occupy premises or the description of a party to a property title.

Term: The time length of a loan.

Vacancy: Period of time a property is without a tenant.

Valuation: Assessment of the value of a property given in a written report by a registered valuer.

Valuer: A person licensed to give an estimation of the value of property.

Variable rate loan: A home loan for which the interest rate changes as the money market changes.

Vendor: Person offering a property for sale.

Index

Destiny Financial Solutions

Destiny Financial Solutions can assist you with a range of investment needs, as follows:

1 Investment workshops and seminars

Margaret Lomas frequently conducts evening seminars and national workshops. The aim of the seminars is to provide clarity on information contained in Margaret's books and allow attendees the chance to have their personal questions answered.

The workshops will be a full day format at which investing in general will be discussed. This will assist all investors to make wiser choices about their investing future. Attendees will receive a workshop manual and an investor pack. To express your interest in attending either a workshop or a seminar, phone 1800 648 640 or email us at **workshop@edestiny.com.au**. Watch the website for more information about all Destiny events.

2 Personal support and assistance

Destiny Financial Solutions is expanding its network to provide personal assistance by trained branch staff in many areas throughout Australia. We can assist you to put together a personalised property investing strategy which is not reliant on the purchase of particular property. All of our branches offer financial advising support and assistance for direct property investors. Phone or email us, or visit the website to find out our branch locations or to ask about the unique services we can offer.

3   Free download

Phone 1800 648 640 or email us at **download@edestiny.com.au** for instructions.

4   Positive cash flow property register

To access property from the Destiny positive cash flow property register, call 1300 551 113, email **pcfpr@edestiny.com.au** for a free listing, or visit our website. Note that this service is independent of Destiny Financial Solutions financial advising services, and is free to all readers.

5   Join the Destiny team

Exciting business opportunities exist for enthusiastic people to join Margaret's team. Visit the website for more information on these opportunities.

Thank you for reading this book. We can be contacted at:
info@edestiny.com.au

For assistance with your finance needs contact:
finance@edestiny.com.au

For download instructions, contact:
download@edestiny.com.au

If you would like to tell us how you felt about this book, or make a suggestion for future books, please contact:
margaret.lomas@edestiny.com.au

Destiny Financial Solutions Pty Ltd
PO Box 5400
Chittaway Bay NSW 2261
Ph: 1800 648 640
www.edestiny.com.au

ALSO BY MARGARET LOMAS

HOW TO CREATE AN INCOME FOR LIFE

Margaret's key to long-term wealth creation is a unique approach she and her husband have followed themselves, with proven success, for years. These pages are not full of hyped-up theory and get-rich-quick promises, but contain a step-by-step, easy-to-follow positive cash flow investment strategy that almost anyone can adopt to create an income for life.

In her easy-to-read engaging style, Margaret offers useful information on:

- ❐ Safely investing in positive cash flow property.
- ❐ Taking advantage of home equity and hedging against the usual pitfalls of investing in property.
- ❐ Employing a specific borrowing strategy which eliminates debt quickly.
- ❐ The questions to ask when researching your market.
- ❐ Following strict, unemotional guidelines for investment property selection.

From the author

Just when I think I couldn't possibly write another book, into my head floods an abundance of new information and I can't wait to get into my office and start again.

I love writing and it seems to come so easily. I can't write little bits at a time—I have to sit down and bash away until it is done. This usually involves locking myself away for a two-week stretch, appearing only for meals and sleep. The main problem I have at present is deciding what not to write!

The other problem I have is time. I have 120 new ideas each day but only time for about 50 or 60 of them. I either need to be cloned, made younger (to give me more time on this earth) or to find the serum for eternal youth so I can stick around a bit longer.

I don't mean to make out I have this wonderful life. It can be amazing how you can achieve so much through hard work and dedication, and then have everyone say how 'lucky' you are. Well, let me tell you that I am not lucky and nor do I live a charmed life—I certainly have just as many negatives in my life as everyone else. The difference, I believe, is in how you look at things. I always look ahead—this way any problems are quickly dispensed with and I am looking forward to the next challenge.

You can get ahead too, simply by ignoring what others say about you, not worrying what anyone thinks, and listening to your instincts. You have one chance at this life, so choose today to make the most of yours by getting out there and doing everything you possibly can to make your time on earth as effective as possible, for you and for everyone else around you.

Live, learn and love those around you. Life is great, but only if you choose for it to be!

Acknowledgments

To say that the staff at Destiny have done a mammoth job would be the understatement of the year. With two new books in 2002, as well as television stories and radio interviews, we have been inundated, and frankly I am surprised that all my staff didn't just resign!

Teresa—our longest serving staff member and the rock. Without Teresa there would be no Destiny. She can never leave!

Renee—we did warn you! You have proven that age is not an issue and you have provided an excellent standard of service to our branches.

Susan and Juliette—without whom the property register would still be a dream. Your dedication is unsurpassed and you both deserve the success you are experiencing.

My branch managers—Steve and Helen, Laurel and Michael, Lynn, and all those involved with the branches. Thank you for helping me promote our message to our clients with such care and consideration. Destiny is you.

Tom Plenty from BMT and Associates for his valuable help with depreciation issues, Egon Grossberg from Grossberg Partners, Melbourne, for the information about property structures and anyone else whose brain I picked.

And Reuben. I love you. You never let me down. Your words of encouragement help me soar above the rest and ensure that I never doubt my abilities. Without you, I would have and be nothing. Thank you.